Ollie O

WRITE A NOVEL BEFORE YOU TURN 13 WORKBOOK

45 Writing Prompts and Exercises to Help You Write and Finish a Novel

Illustrations by Alejandro Miranda

ISBN 978-1-990828-01-0

CalamariTales.com

CONTENTS

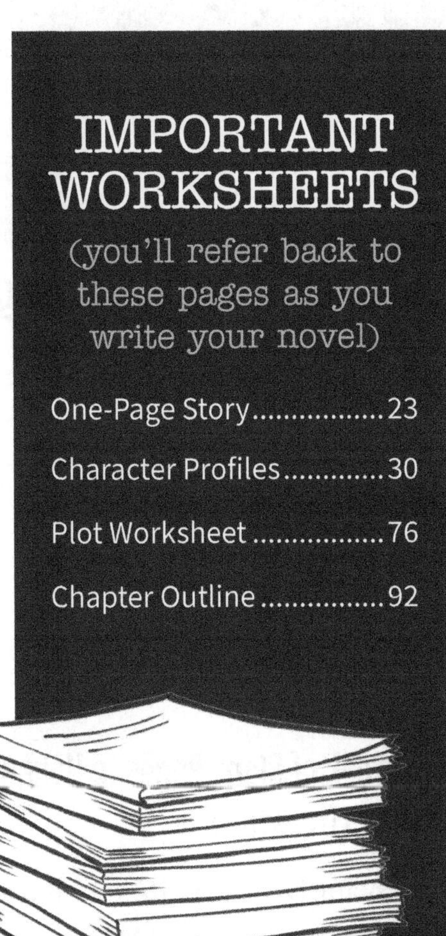

IMPORTANT WORKSHEETS
(you'll refer back to these pages as you write your novel)

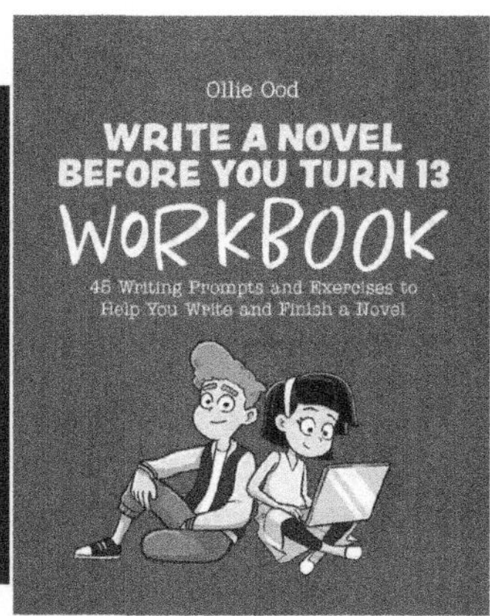

FREE DOWNLOAD!

If you need extra copies of some of the worksheets found in this book, go to CalamariTales.com/novel-worksheets to download your free pdf.

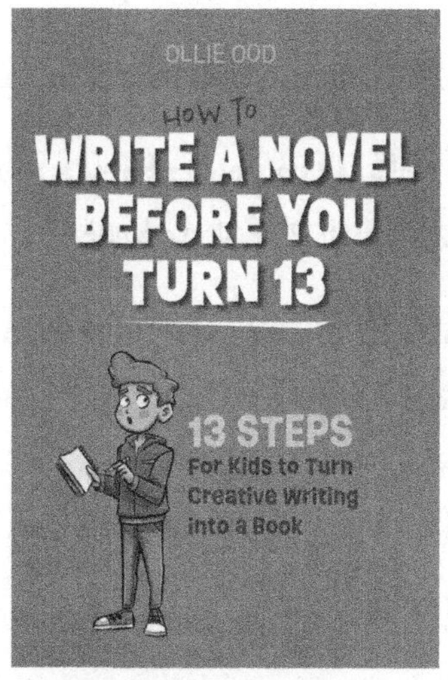

Learn even more about writing!

If you're looking for more resources, check out *How to Write a Novel Before You Turn 13*—it's a reference book that takes you through the 13 steps in greater detail. Available on Amazon.

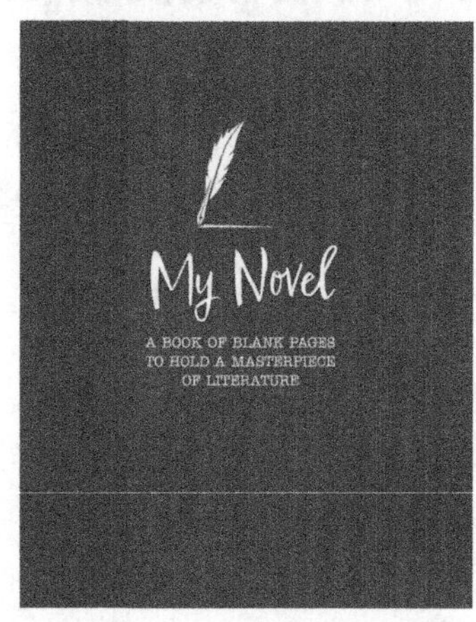

MY NOVEL: A Book of Blank Pages to Hold a Masterpiece of Literature

If you need a blank book to write your novel in, check out *My Novel*. It's got 120 lined pages, plus an appendix of worksheets to help you develop your story. Available on Amazon.

Introduction

IF YOU'RE THINKING, *"I have a lot of ideas, but I don't know where to begin to write a novel"* you've picked up the right book!

Writing a novel is a big task, like running a marathon. It can feel impossible! But the truth is, with work and determination, it *is* possible. Kids just like you have done it before.

Did you know there are novels, right now, in *your* library that were written by kids? That's right! Gordan Korman, who has written more than 90 books for kids and teens, wrote his first book in the 7th grade! At the age of 15, Christopher Paolini wrote his book *Eragon,* which went on to be a *New York Times* Bestseller.

If you want to write a novel, you start with small steps. Just like no one goes from eating potato chips on their couch every day to running the Boston marathon, you can't jump straight from story idea to finished novel.

There's a path to follow, laid out by writers who have done it before.

Useful tools

Pencil or pen
You'll be doing a lot of writing!

Red pen
This will be handy for the editing exercises.

Timer
Some of the exercises are timed.

Favorite chapter book(s)
Some exercises will ask you to find reference examples in your favorite books.

Notebook or computer
This book has a lot of pages for you to write different scenes from your book, but you'll need more space to write your whole novel.

How to use this book

This book is meant to be used, written in, doodled on, underlined, thrown into your backpack, and whatever else you want to do with it!

If possible, it's best to work beginning to end since some of the exercises build upon each other.

There is room in the workbook to do the exercises and brainstorm, but when you start writing your novel, you'll need a separate notebook or a computer. You can write with pen and paper, pencil and paper, or type your first draft on the computer. You'll find what works best for you!

Remember, everything you see in this workbook is advice and guidance, but you are the writer, and you can (and will) find the way that you prefer to write and create stories. Some methods are easier than others, but there is no wrong way to do it!

13 STEPS

Writing a novel is a big project, but it can be broken down into 13 easy-to-follow steps. Each step has prompts and exercises that will get you closer to having a complete novel.

YOU CAN DO THIS!

13 STEPS
TO WRITE YOUR NOVEL

Listen to your creative ideas
Listen to your imagination and find your story idea.

Build your foundation
Take your idea and transform it into a one-page story.

Create character profiles
Get to know the characters who will star in your story.

Choose your point of view (POV)
Choose who is telling the story.

Decide on locations and settings
Decide where and when your story will take place.

Plan your story's plot
Plan out all the events in your novel.

 ## Divide your plot into chapters

Create the building blocks for a full novel.

 ## Set up some action

Add the elements that make a lively and dynamic story.

 ## Write great dialogue

Discover how to make your characters speak.

 ## Build to the climax

Mix together all the tension and action you've been creating.

 ## Resolve your story

Tie up all the loose ends.

 ## Revise and edit

Take a good story and make it great

 ## Publish your book

Turn your manuscript into a real book.

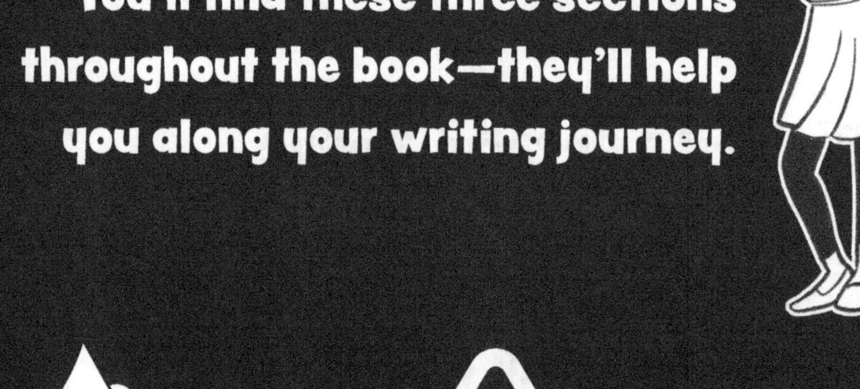

These are short, informative sections to give you the knowledge to complete the writing prompts and worksheets. These tips provide essential information about writing stories and definitions of the common words used in the writing exercises.

The "Watch Out!" sections help you avoid common pitfalls that new writers often fall into. There are many snares and traps along the way when writing a story this large, but these helpful tips are here to help you avoid those common mistakes.

These sections are full of writing prompts, brainstorming ideas, and exercises to help you get what's in your head onto the page. Try not to skip any! Part of being a writer is developing the discipline to write even when you'd rather be watching YouTube.

STEP 1
LISTEN TO YOUR CREATIVE IDEAS

TIPS TO KNOW

BEFORE YOU CAN write a novel, you need a story idea. Story-making is just imagining *what* happens and coming up with plausible reasons *why* it happens.

Did you know you have already made up thousands of stories in your life? Our brains make up stories every time we wonder about things—why your mom is grumpy, who ate all the cookies, what dogs think about.

If you don't have an idea yet, take some time to let yourself wonder. Lie in the grass. Ride your bike. Stare at the rain through the window.

WATCH OUT!

HAVE YOU EVER tried to write something but found yourself getting frustrated and thinking, "What a stupid idea!" Remember, it's easy to be too harsh to your ideas. Don't be mean to your thoughts, or they'll stop coming! Ideas don't have to be *good enough*—just let your ideas exist. Write down everything and anything that comes. You can sort them out later.

3 minutes...

1. Turn on your creativity

TAKE THIS BOOK and a timer, and go sit somewhere quiet and relaxing (maybe on your bed or outside in the grass). Set the timer for three minutes. Write everything that comes into your mind for three minutes straight. Try not to think, just write! Keep your hand moving. Write everything you notice or wonder about. If you get stuck, think of the four senses: touch, smell, hear, and taste.

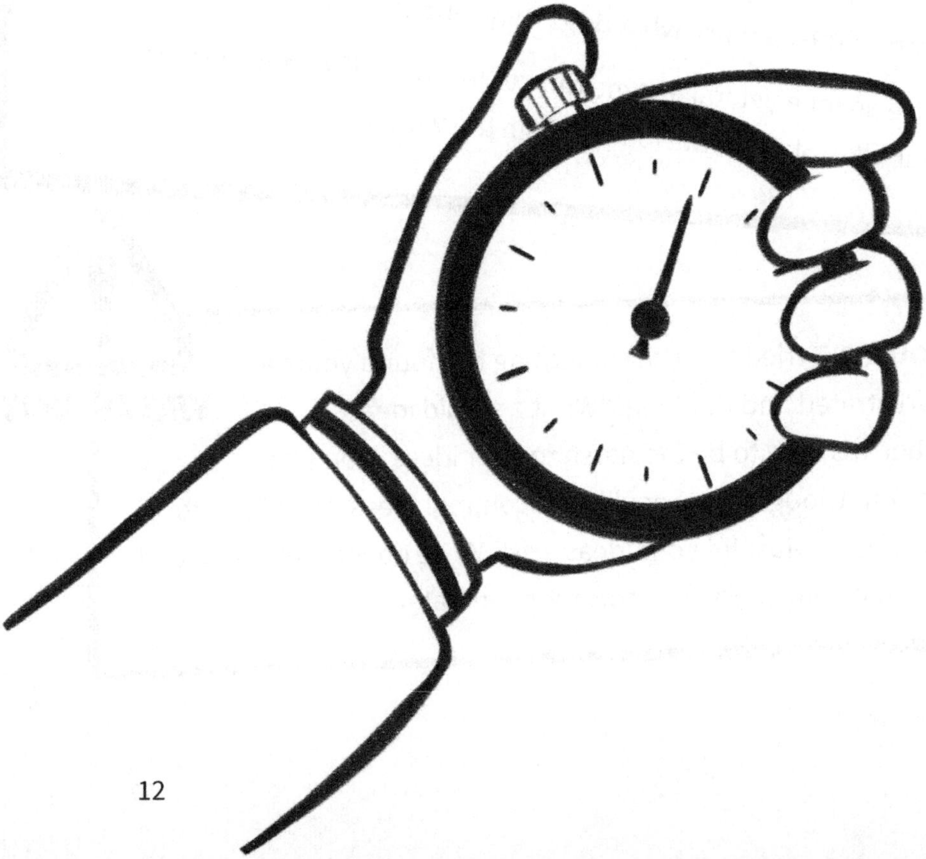

1 minute

2 minutes

3 minutes

2. Finding the story seeds

PICK ONE ITEM from the last exercise and see if you can find the seeds of a story. If you noticed the grass was itchy, can you make up a creative reason the grass is itchy? What if people are becoming more allergic to the outside because they are inside on screens all day? What if one kid realizes this and has to make everyone believe them? Try to turn your observations into the origins of a story.

3. I don't get it!

WRITE A PARAGRAPH about something you don't understand. Maybe it's how microwaves work, or perhaps it's why a person acts the way they do. Describe what you don't understand, and then come up with five reasons that might be explanations. These don't have to make sense! The crazier, the better. Did you come up with something that would make a good story?

____

____

____

____

____

____

Possible explanations:

1 _______________________________________

2 _______________________________________

3 _______________________________________

4 _______________________________________

5 _______________________________________

4. The 2-thing mashup

YOU MAY BE feeling stuck and having a hard time getting an idea. The great thing is, two ordinary things mashed together can make something unusual and fun. What if one normal thing (like a kid) found themselves in an unusual situation (like being in charge of a zoo)?

Take something *usual* and mash it with something *unusual* (like a place, purpose, or quality). Write as much as you can about it. Keep asking questions and try to answer them. What would happen if this mashup occurred in your story? What would that mean for your character/how would it change their world? Would it cause any new problems?

math class

learns to fly

family dog

shifts into a new reality

5. Turn your idea into a question

DO YOU ALREADY have an idea you'd like to turn into a novel? Great! Take your story idea and see if you can turn it into a question like "What if…." For instance, if I were making a story idea for *The Wizard of Oz*, I would say, "What if a girl from Kansas, who longs for something more, finds herself in a magical land?" Can you turn your idea into a question? Framing your idea as a question will help you start to think about what happens in your idea. This is important because events, action, and problems change an idea into a story.

what if a lonely boy finds out he's a wizard ?

what if a pig befriends a spider who saves his life ?

Once you've done that, try to ask other questions, related to the ones on the previous page. Don't worry about the answers for this exercise!

How does the lonely boy deal with being a wizard?

What can he do and not do as a wizard?

How can a spider be friends with a pig?

How does the spider save the pig's life?

STEP 2
BUILD YOUR FOUNDATION

TIPS TO KNOW

LET'S TAKE THAT STORY idea and turn it into a one-page story. You may be thinking, "A one-page story?! I want to write a novel!" I know, I know, and I promise we'll get there. But before you can write a novel, you need to understand the story you want to tell.

REMEMBER I SAID I would warn you about common traps new writers fall into? Starting to write your novel before you have a basic idea of your story is one of them. At the very least, you need to know who your story is about and why it matters to them. It can be helpful to know more, such as what happens in your story.

WATCH OUT!

Doing this "pre-writing" work can save you many headaches in the end! In the middle of writing their novel, nobody likes to find out that they don't know what should happen next or what the first half is actually about. If YOU don't know your story, how do you expect other people to understand it? But fear not—you can do this! Just remember, there are no shortcuts to writing a great novel.

1. Develop your one-page story

THIS STORY SHOULD be brief and just tell the facts of what happens, who your characters are, and what the problem is they are trying to solve. Use the brainstorming you started in the last section and make some notes that answer some of the questions you asked in the last exercise.

- ____
- ____
- ____
- ____
- ____
- ____
- ____
- ____
- ____
- ____

2. Write your one-page story

THIS ONE-PAGE STORY will guide you as you build the rest of the novel.

After you've written it, look it over.

👉 **Have you given your characters something they want or need?**

👉 **Have you created something or someone standing in their way from getting it?**

👉 **What can you throw into your character's way to make it harder to reach their goal?**

👉 **What does your main character want in your story most of all?**

Once you have answered these questions—and it might not be until you're further along in the writing process—go back and revise your one-page story.

STEP 3
CREATE CHARACTER PROFILES

CHARACTERS ARE THE PEOPLE (or animals, or aliens) living and acting out your story. In the story of your life, you're not just a character—you're the main character! The main character is the person the story is really about. Other people and animals or creatures might make an appearance, but they are secondary characters. Ultimately, the story is about the main character (what they do, what they care about, how they grow). This is their story and no one else's!

What your main character wants is the most important thing to know. Each character must want something in the story, and your main character's want or need will be the driving force behind how they act and what they do.

The more you get to know your character, the easier it will be to write them!

IMPORTANT! The only character details that need to show up in your story are the relevant ones. I can't stress this enough! Many stories are weighed down by unnecessary information, such as a character got braces in the fourth grade and their favorite animal is the elephant. Unless your plot focuses on these details somehow, your readers DON'T NEED TO KNOW THIS. This exercise is for you to envision your character as real as possible.

1. Writing the main character

NOT ALL CHARACTERS have what it takes to be an excellent main character. Your main character is essential. If you hope anyone likes your book, they have to win over your readers.

So, what makes a great main character? There are three qualities:

☞ **Someone active**
   (they are in charge of their story)

☞ **Someone interesting**
   (they have unique or special qualities that draw readers in)

☞ **Someone likable**
   (they show us their weaknesses and strengths, and we connect to them)

WRITE A LIST of your favorite three main characters from books or movies. Then, think about why you like them? What qualities do you admire? What weaknesses do they have?

Main character #1:	Main character #2:	Main character #3:
Good qualities:	Good qualities:	Good qualities:
Weaknesses:	Weaknesses:	Weaknesses:

2. Fill out character profiles

Before filling out the character profiles on the next pages, you may want to make copies of the worksheets.

MAIN CHARACTER PROFILE

MAIN CHARACTER PROFILE

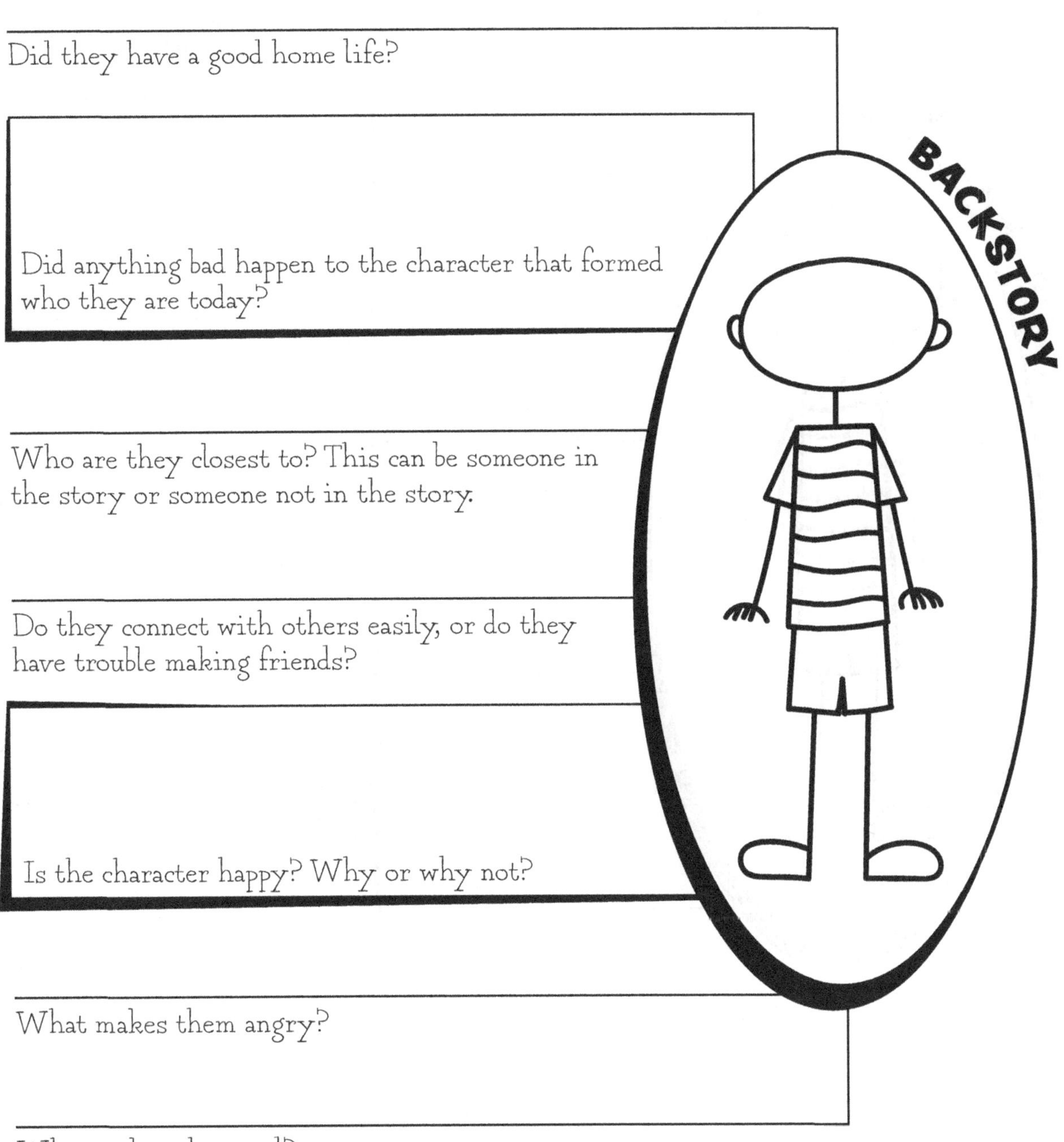

Did they have a good home life?

Did anything bad happen to the character that formed who they are today?

Who are they closest to? This can be someone in the story or someone not in the story.

Do they connect with others easily, or do they have trouble making friends?

Is the character happy? Why or why not?

What makes them angry?

What makes them sad?

MAIN CHARACTER PROFILE

Evidence How will you show the character trait in the story?

Character Trait
(good or bad)

Character Trait
(good or bad)

Character Trait
(good or bad)

Character Trait
(good or bad)

Describe your character in one sentence:

____

____

MAIN CHARACTER PROFILE

How does this character see themself? Do they feel smart, dumb, strong, weak, brave, cowardly, etc.

____

____

____

____

How do others see this character?

____

____

____

____

Is there anything unusual about their behavior?

____

____

The character's part in the story

How/When will this character be introduced into your story?

____

____

____

What does your character want most in the story? Be as specific as possible:

____

____

____

How does your character go after what they want? What actions do they take to get what they want? If they don't go after it, why not?

____

____

____

How do the events of the story change this character's personality or circumstance?

____

____

2ND CHARACTER PROFILE

2ND CHARACTER PROFILE

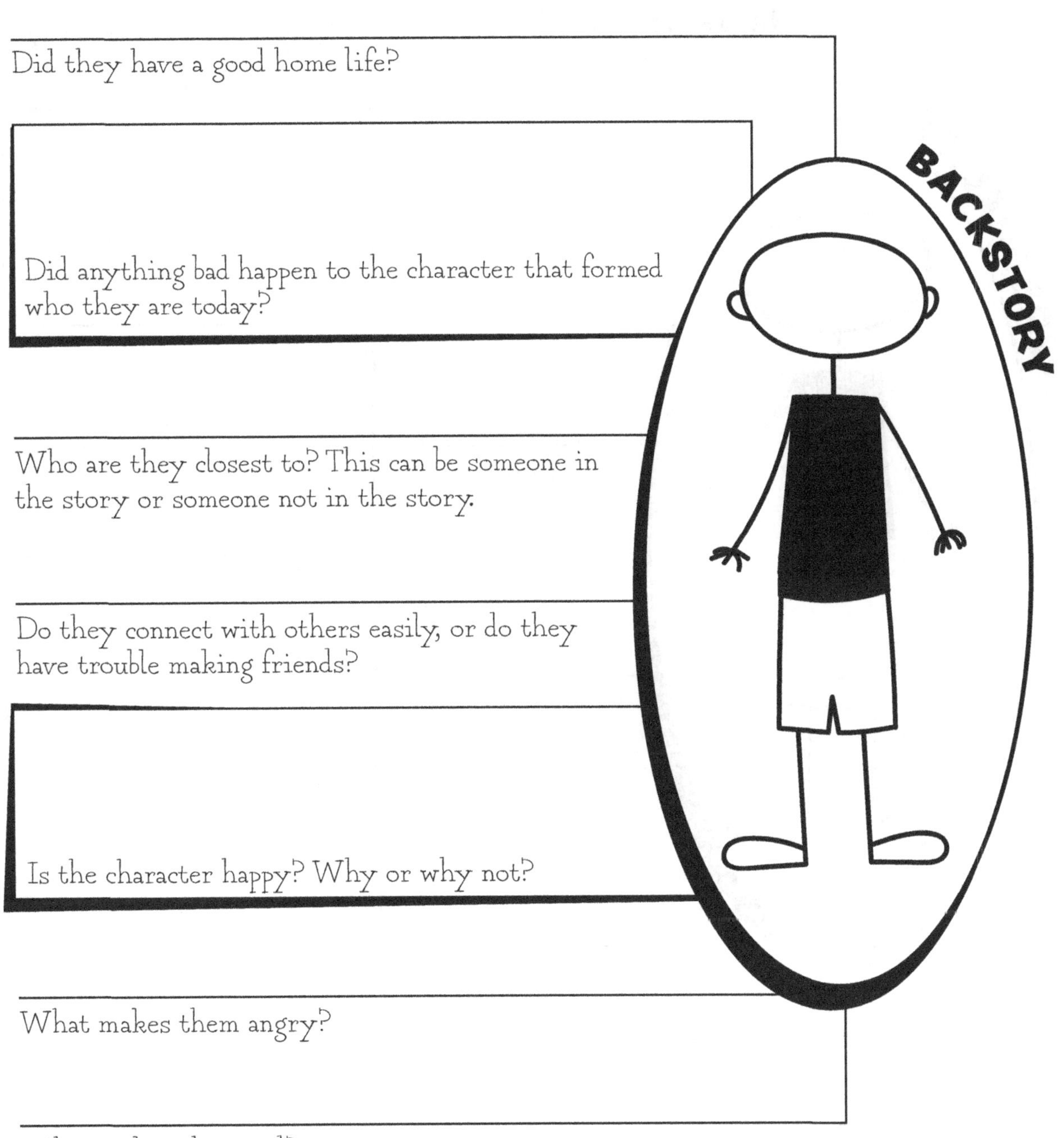

Did they have a good home life?

Did anything bad happen to the character that formed who they are today?

Who are they closest to? This can be someone in the story or someone not in the story.

Do they connect with others easily, or do they have trouble making friends?

Is the character happy? Why or why not?

What makes them angry?

What makes them sad?

2ND CHARACTER PROFILE

Evidence How will you show the character trait in the story?

PERSONALITY

Character Trait
(good or bad)

Character Trait
(good or bad)

Character Trait
(good or bad)

Character Trait
(good or bad)

Describe your character in one sentence:

2ND CHARACTER PROFILE

How does this character see themself? Do they feel smart, dumb, strong, weak, brave, cowardly, etc.

____

____

____

____

How do others see this character?

____

____

____

____

Is there anything unusual about their behavior?

____

The character's part in the story

How will this character be introduced?

____

____

____

What does your character want most in the story? Is it the same as the main character? The opposite?

____

____

How does your character go after what they want?

____

____

How do the events of the story change this character's personality or circumstance?

____

____

How is this character connected to the main character?

____

3RD CHARACTER PROFILE

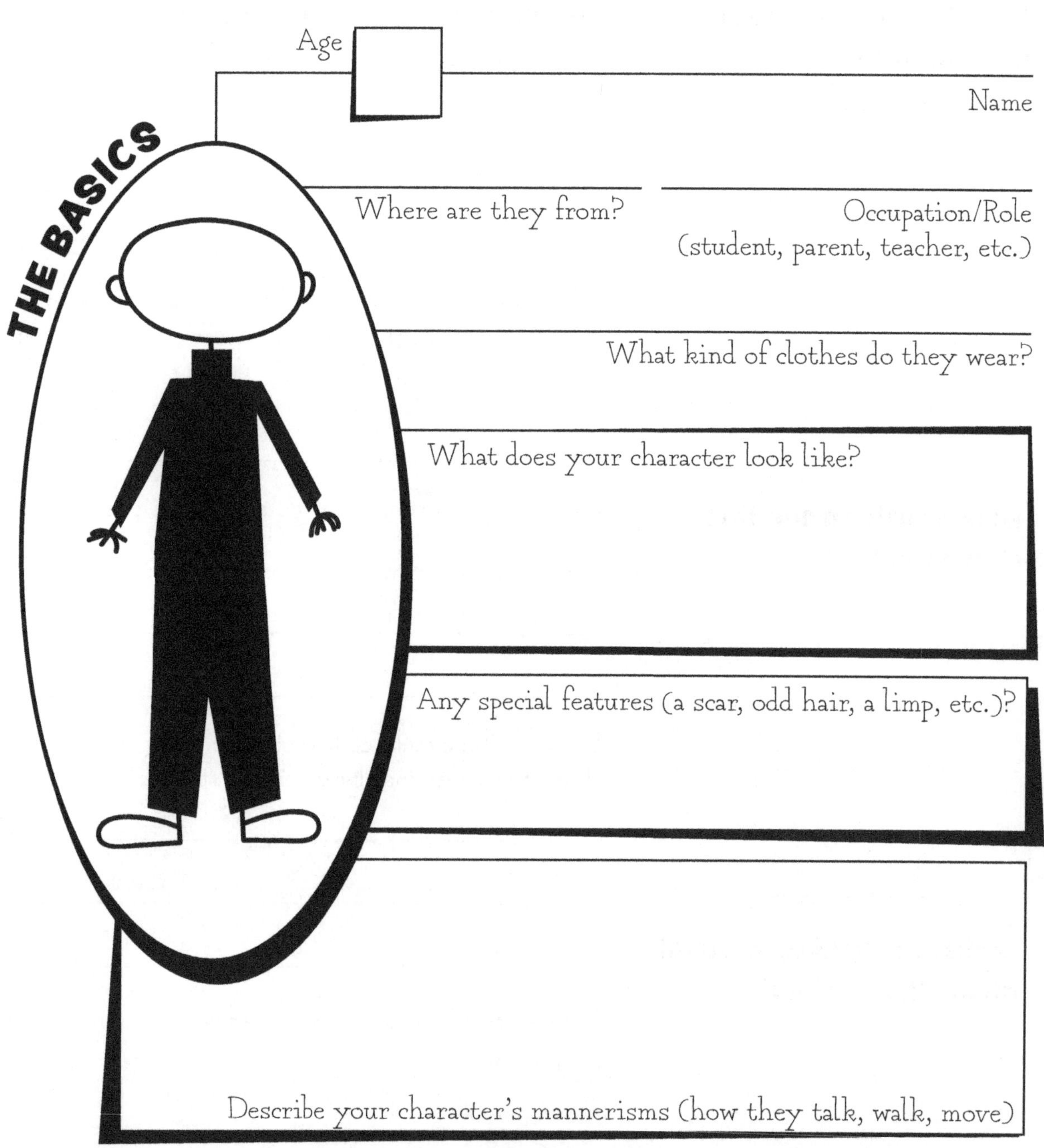

3RD CHARACTER PROFILE

Did they have a good home life?

Did anything bad happen to the character that formed who they are today?

Who are they closest to? This can be someone in the story or someone not in the story.

Do they connect with others easily, or do they have trouble making friends?

Is the character happy? Why or why not?

What makes them angry?

What makes them sad?

3RD CHARACTER PROFILE

Evidence How will you show the character trait in the story?

PERSONALITY

Character Trait
(good or bad)

Character Trait
(good or bad)

Character Trait
(good or bad)

Character Trait
(good or bad)

Describe your character in one sentence:

3RD CHARACTER PROFILE

How does this character see themself? Do they feel smart, dumb, strong, weak, brave, cowardly, etc.

____

____

____

____

How do others see this character?

____

____

____

Is there anything unusual about their behavior?

____

The character's part in the story

How will this character be introduced?

____

____

What does your character want most in the story? Is it the same as the main character? The opposite?

____

____

How does your character go after what they want?

____

____

How do the events of the story change this character's personality or circumstance?

____

____

How is this character connected to the main character?

____

4TH CHARACTER PROFILE

4TH CHARACTER PROFILE

Did they have a good home life?

Did anything bad happen to the character that formed who they are today?

Who are they closest to? This can be someone in the story or someone not in the story.

Do they connect with others easily, or do they have trouble making friends?

Is the character happy? Why or why not?

What makes them angry?

What makes them sad?

4TH CHARACTER PROFILE

Evidence How will you show the character trait in the story?

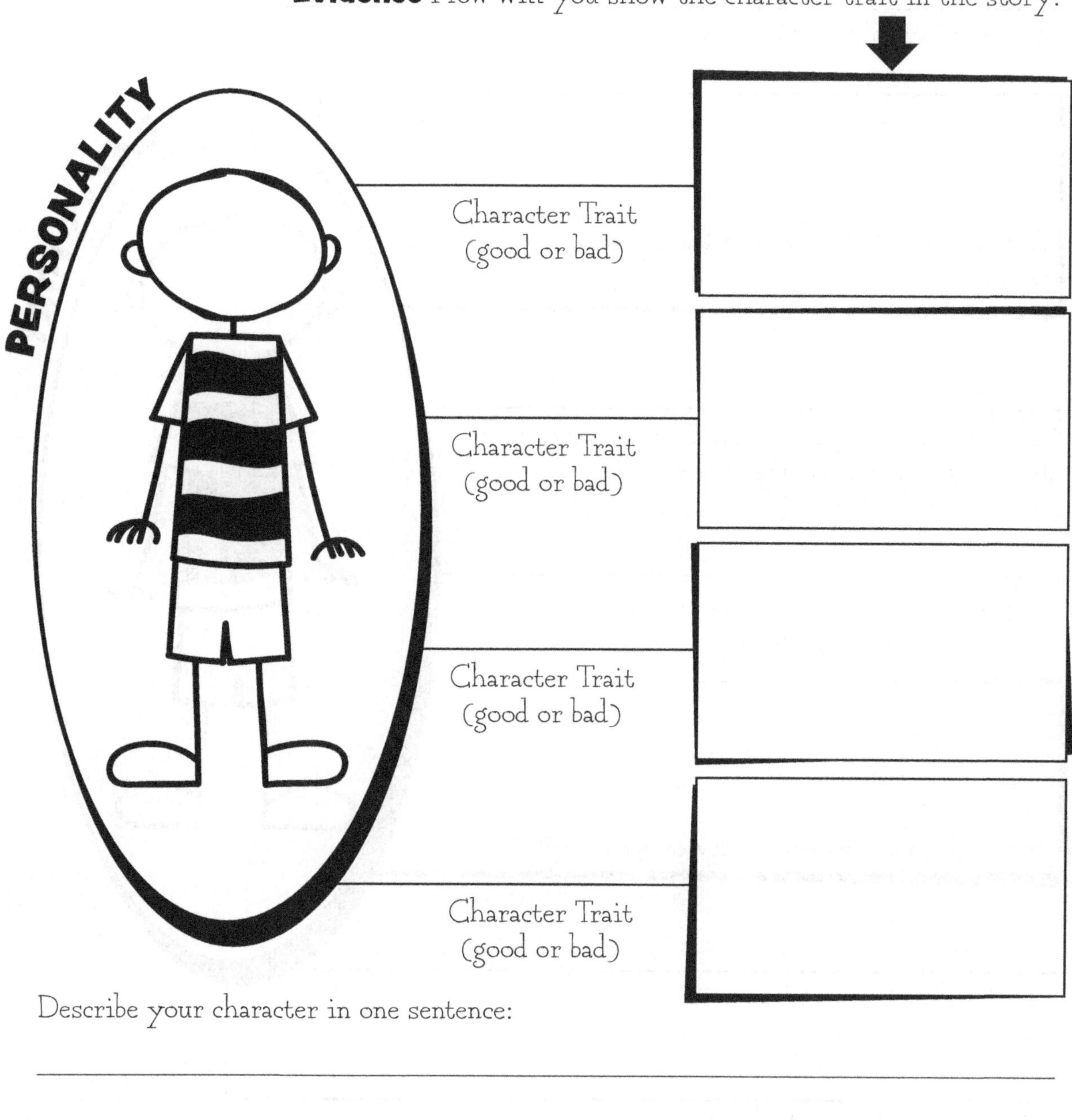

Describe your character in one sentence:

____

____

4TH CHARACTER PROFILE

How does this character see themself? Do they feel smart, dumb, strong, weak, brave, cowardly, etc.

____

____

____

How do others see this character?

____

____

____

Is there anything unusual about their behavior?

____

____

The character's part in the story

How will this character be introduced?

____

____

What does your character want most in the story? Is it the same as the main character? The opposite?

____

How does your character go after what they want?

____

____

How do the events of the story change this character's personality or circumstance?

____

____

How is this character connected to the main character?

____

CHARACTER NOTES

POV CHART

WHAT POINT OF VIEW IS IT?

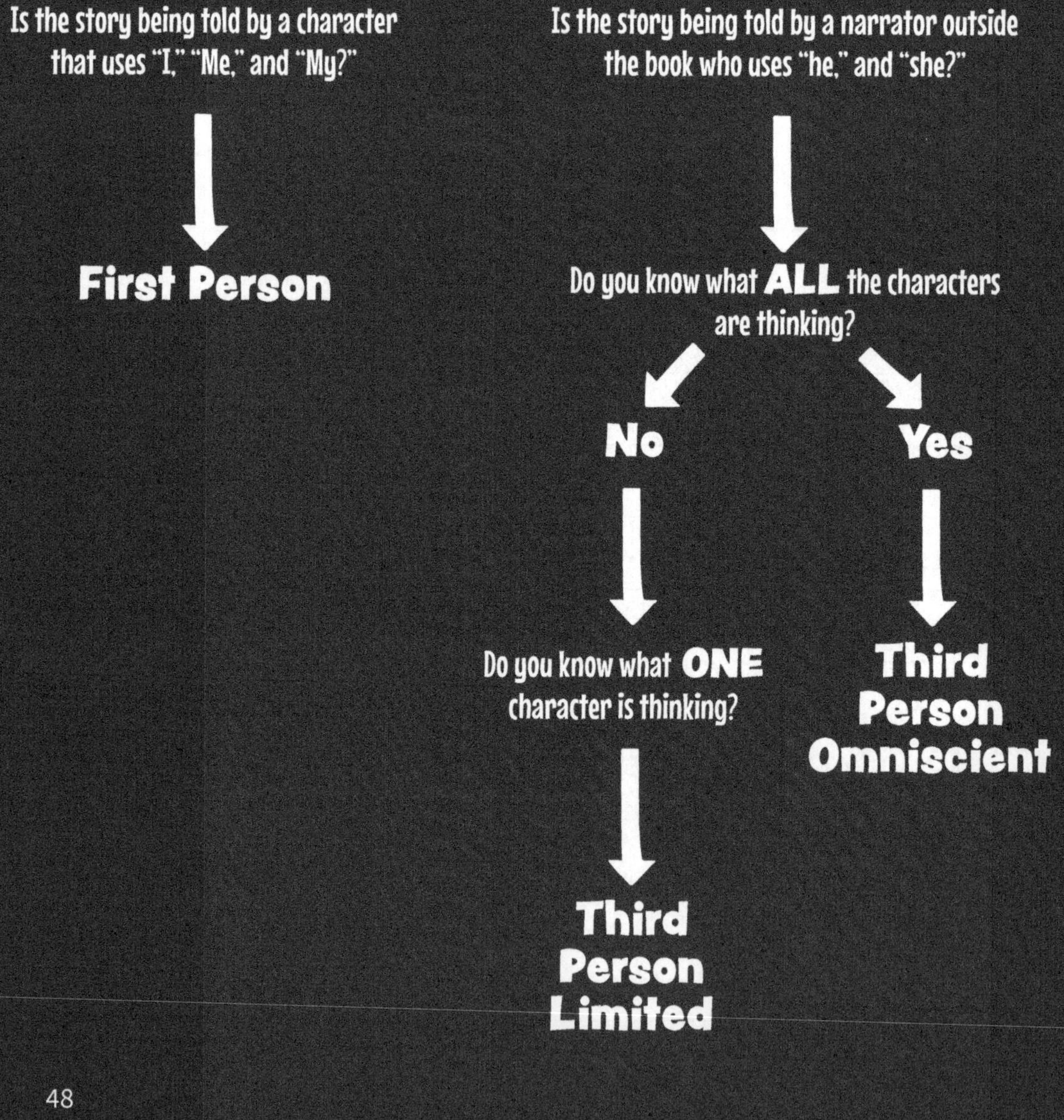

Is the story being told by a character that uses "I," "Me," and "My?"

↓

First Person

Is the story being told by a narrator outside the book who uses "he," and "she?"

↓

Do you know what **ALL** the characters are thinking?

No / **Yes**

Do you know what **ONE** character is thinking?

↓

Third Person Limited

Third Person Omniscient

STEP 4
CHOOSE YOUR POINT OF VIEW

POINT OF VIEW, OR POV, is the perspective the story is being told from. If you're looking down from way up high, we often say you are looking from a bird's eye view. We could also say you're looking from a bird's point of view. Some POVs are distant and far away, and some are close up.

There are three main POVs that you need to know in creative writing:

First Person

A character in the story, usually the main character, tells us the story and relates their experiences. *(Pronouns used are I, Me, and My).*

Third Person Limited

An outside narrator, not a character, tells us the story, and we are limited to what **ONE CHARACTER** can see. We can also see inside that character's head and thoughts. *(Pronouns used are She/He, Her/His).*

Third Person Omniscient

An outside narrator, not a character, tells us the story and **IS NOT LIMITED** to just one character. They can see and know all the thoughts of **ALL THE CHARACTERS**. Usually, we stay with one POV person per scene to avoid confusion. *(Pronouns used are She/He, Her/His, They/Them).*

Let's look at an example of the different POVs from the fairytale "Snow White."

told by Snow White

First Person

I couldn't believe **I** was lost so deep in the woods! The sun was setting, and wolves howled out their hunger into the darkness. **I** was just about to give up hope when **I** stumbled onto a cottage.

A little man was drawing water from the well. **I** cleared my throat so **I** wouldn't startle him, but he still jumped back when he saw **me**.

"Hello," **I said**. "May I please come in? I'm lost and all alone."

The little man smiled and called his friends, all six of them. They instantly welcomed **me** into their little cottage, gave **me** a drink, and were so kind **I** almost forgot all about **my** troubles!

Third Person Limited

Snow White couldn't believe **she** was lost so deep in the woods! The sun was setting, and wolves howled out their hunger into the darkness. **She** was just about to give up hope when **she** stumbled onto a cottage.

A little man was drawing water from the well. **Snow White** cleared **her** throat to get his attention and he jumped back when he saw **her**.

"Hello," **she said**. "May I please come in? I'm lost and all alone."

The little man broke into a smile and called his friends, all six of them. They instantly welcomed **her** into their little cottage, gave **her** a drink, and were so kind **she** almost forgot all about **her** troubles!

Third Person Omniscient

Snow White couldn't believe **she** was lost so deep in the woods! The sun was setting, and wolves howled out their hunger into the darkness. **She** was just about to give up hope when **she** stumbled onto a cottage.

Dopey was drawing water from the well. **He thought he heard someone clear their throat, but he was almost sure he was alone. He looked up and jumped back when he saw a girl staring at him! What in the world is she doing out here all alone? he thought.**

"Hello," **Snow White said**. "May I please come in? I'm lost and all alone." **She hoped the little man was kind.**

Dopey broke into a smile, **relieved that she seemed to be just a girl, and not an ogre—he was terrified of ogres.** He called his friends—all six of them—and they instantly welcomed Snow White into their little cottage and gave her a drink.

Snow White couldn't believe how welcoming all her new friends were. They were so kind she almost forgot all about her troubles.

You can see in this last example how I had to add a few more descriptions and names to keep the reader from getting confused about whose thoughts we were listening to.

THE MOST COMMON POVS are either First Person or Third Person Limited for a new writer. There is no right or wrong choice. Just decide, do you want to tell your story from a character's first-hand perspective (First Person), or would you rather have a narrator tell the story who isn't a character at all (Third Person).

IF YOU CHOOSE to write with a **Third Person Limited POV**, you must stay with your POV character (the one you're limited to)! Say your POV character is Dorothy from *The Wizard of Oz*. You have to stay with her the whole time. You can't suddenly jump to the Wicked Witch's castle and show her plotting to send her monkeys if Dorothy isn't there. We, as the readers, can only see and observe what Dorothy sees and observes.

This also goes for feelings and thoughts too! You can't suddenly say, "The Cowardly Lion felt hungry." How do we know that? We aren't inside him, so we can't know that. However, you *can* say, "Dorothy felt scared. She missed Kansas." She is our POV character, so that's okay. If you want the power to show whatever you want and tell us whatever anyone is feeling, even Toto, then you should write with Third Person Omniscient.

1. Practice First Person POV

WRITE A PARAGRAPH from *The Three Little Pigs* fairytale using the first-person point of view. Become one of the characters and tell the story from their viewpoint.

2. Practice Third Person Limited POV

WRITE A PARAGRAPH from *The Three Little Pigs* fairytale using a third-person narrator who is not a character in the story. Pick one character to "follow around" and stay with. (This is the "limited" part of Third Person Limited). Remember, if this character isn't present in a scene, we can't see what happens! We can only go where the character goes and see what they see.

3. Practice Third Person Omniscient POV

WRITE TWO SHORT SCENES from *The Three Little Pigs* fairytale using
a third-person omniscient narrator who is not a character in the story.
Narrate one scene from the perspective of one character and the second
scene from the perspective of another character. Remember that the
narrator will know what each character is thinking.

4. Pull Out Your One-Page Story

GO BACK AND REREAD your one-page story. What POV did you naturally use? First Person? Third Person? Try rewriting your story with a different POV than the one you chose. Which one do you like the best?

5. It's Time to Choose

CHECK OFF which POV you will use to write your novel.

FIRST PERSON

THIRD PERSON
LIMITED

THIRD PERSON
OMNISCIENT

Find three books that use this point of view and read the first three pages of each of them. Take notes about things you notice about that particular POV.

1st Person	3rd Person Limited	3rd Person Omniscient
Example: *Alexander and the Terrible, Horrible, No-Good, Very Bad Day*	Example: *Harry Potter*	Example: *Little Women*

STEP 5
DECIDE ON LOCATIONS AND SETTINGS

TIPS TO KNOW

THE SETTING OF YOUR STORY refers to where and when your story takes place. Your job is to describe your setting in a way that lets your readers imagine the world you are creating and enter into it. You can change a generic "jungle" to a steamy, vine-covered Amazon forest with sloths hanging from the branches through your description and details. The right details help to paint the picture in your readers' minds.

WHEN DESCRIBING YOUR SETTING, pick the best of your details, just a few. Nothing is more boring than paragraphs and paragraphs of description about the setting! We just need a little bit to ground the story, and your reader's brains will fill in the rest.

WATCH OUT!

1. Find Your Setting

Answer the following questions:

What setting does your story take place in? Is it a specific town, a real place, or is your setting more general, such as on an island or a farm?

____

____

Does your story occur in contemporary times (right now) or long ago (sometime in history)? What time of year is it?

____

Are there any "rules" to your world that your readers need to know? (This is good to know if you write fantasy or science fiction).

____

____

What mood would you use to describe your setting? For example, a cabin in the woods could be described as "lonely," and make readers feel fear, where the same cabin could be described as "cozy," and make readers feel happy. What mood do you want your story to have?

____

____

2. Enter Your World

WRITE A SCENE from your first chapter. As you write, picture yourself as your main character, feeling what they feel. Enter into the world completely. What do you notice? What does it feel like, look like, taste like, smell like, sound like? You don't have to show your reader all the senses, but think about what is important to know to experience your world.

3. Learn from the Best

Take a book that you love and find exciting to read. Read the first three
pages. Write down every time the author describes the setting. It might
be that it was night, or a house was old, or that the planet's dirt looked
red. Look how they chose the relevant details.

Book title: ____

- ____

- ____

- ____

- ____

- ____

- ____

- ____

- ____

- ____

- ____

- ____

- ____

- ____

STEP 6
PLAN YOUR STORY'S PLOT

THE PLOT OF YOUR NOVEL is the events that happen—the choices your characters make, the betrayals, the escapes, the successes, the mistakes. These all make up the plot of your story. And the action of the novel is all propelled along by what your main character wants—their goal.

You will keep your character going forward, trying and failing and trying again to achieve their goal.

BEFORE WE GO ANY FURTHER, we need to talk about structure. This is the framework that your story is built on. You can't think about the plot of your book and what will happen in it until you understand the story structure.

One of the most straightforward story structures is the three-act structure. In its simplest form, it is:

Act 1 = Beginning
Act 2 = Middle
Act 3 = End

Within each of these acts, you will find plot points. "Plot points" are the crucial moments where something changes or shifts the story in a new direction.

This book uses a plot worksheet to help figure out the plot points in each act and ensure your story has all the components of a well-told tale.

The first plot point to think about is the "Inciting Incident." The Inciting Incident is often something that happens or new information your main character learns that launches them into the story's main events. It surprises the protagonist (main character) and could be a new problem or opportunity.

SIDE-NOTE—the antagonist is your main villain in the story.

ACT 1

Opening

Here, we introduce the protagonist (or main characters) and give the readers a feel for what kind of story it will be.

Setup

This section introduces the story's other essential side characters.

Inciting Incident

This event launches the main events of the story.

Call to Action

There is an opportunity for the main character to make a choice.

ACT 2

The Choice

The main characters make active choices as they move forward to reach what they want.

Try/Fail

The protagonist and friends/sidekicks try to solve their problems. They fail a lot but have some successes as they move toward the story goal.

Midpoint

Some unexpected revelation sends the story in a new direction. For the first time in the story, the protagonist may doubt if they can do this.

Attack and Bad Guys Regroup

The protagonist tries to carry on but the bad guys now see them as a serious threat and ramp up their attacks.

Dark Moment

Things are the worst they've ever been. The protagonist loses hope and nearly gives up.

ACT 3

Turning Point

Something offers hope (a new idea, lucky break, an unseen friend comes through). The protagonist decides to keep going.

A New Plan

Energized by the new info or energy from the Turning Point, the protagonist forms a new plan to reach the story goal.

Climax

This is the big moment of the whole story. The protagonist and team give their all to reach their goal and defeat any antagonists.

Resolution

After the Climax, this is a period of resolving any unfinished parts of your story and returning to a new normal.

Now let's learn how to use the plot worksheet to create your story. For an example, I have used *The Wizard of Oz* to fill out the worksheet with a familiar story. I am using the account from the 1939 film.

Opening

Here we introduce the protagonist or main character and give the readers a feel for what kind of story it will be and offer a "hook." The hook is some interesting or intriguing scene that will catch the readers, like a fish on a hook, so they won't want to put the book down.

Setup

This section introduces the world's other important characters (such as friends or enemies) and hints at the conflict.

Inciting Incident

This event launches the main events of the story. It comes as a surprise to the protagonist and could be a new problem or opportunity.

Call to Action

After the Inciting Incident, the protagonist must react to the new reality. What will the character do as a result of the Inciting Incident? What is their story goal, or the main thing they now want?

We see Dorothy at her farm in Kansas and learn that she longs for something different. She's a dreamer. And she wants to be appreciated and noticed.

Dorothy wanders the farm and interacts with the farmhands and Auntie Em. We also see her enemy, Mrs. Gulch, who threatens to take Toto and then returns with the police to take him. Dorothy yells at her.

When Toto escapes and returns, Dorothy decides to run away from home to keep him safe. She comes across a traveling gypsy psychic and asks to join him on adventures.

Dorothy wants to go on the road, but even this short trip has taught her she misses home. The psychic tells her that he sees the future, and Auntie Em misses her terribly. Dorothy realizes she loves her home and decides to go back. Unfortunately, just as Dorothy gets home, a tornado comes. She hits her head and dreams the tornado lifts her house to Oz.

ACT 2

PART ONE

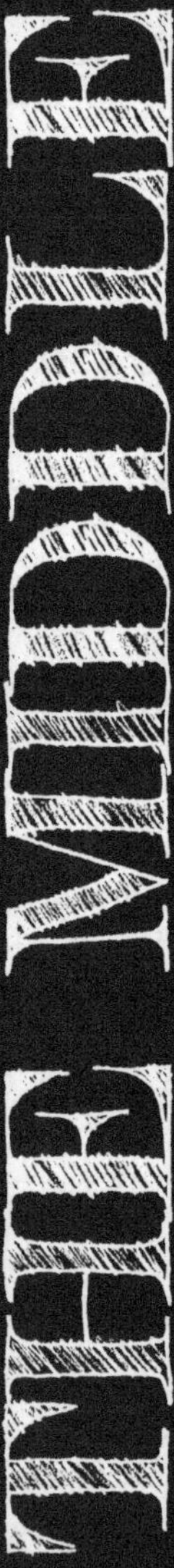

The Choice

The protagonist makes active choices as they move forward, trying to reach their story goal.

Try/Fail

The protagonist and friends/sidekicks try to solve their problems. They fail a lot but have some successes as they move toward the story goal.

Midpoint/Reversal

Some unexpected revelation sends the story in a new direction, raising the stakes. For the first time in the story, the protagonist may doubt if they can do this.

Dorothy decides to keep the ruby slippers (making an enemy of the Wicked Witch) and journey to the Emerald City to see the Wizard.

Dorothy meets friends along the way who she decides to help and who will help her on the journey. They also encounter setbacks from the Wicked Witch.

The group finally makes it to the Emerald City only to learn the Wizard won't see them. When he finally does, he won't help them unless they bring him the broom of the Wicked Witch.

Attack and Bad Guys Regroup

The protagonist tries to carry on but the bad guys now see them as a serious threat and ramp up their attacks.

Dark Moment

Things are the worst they've ever been. The protagonist loses hope and nearly gives up. There seems to be no way forward.

Turning Point

Something offers hope (a new idea, lucky break, an unseen friend comes through). The protagonist decides to keep going.

Dorothy and her friends are attacked on the way to the Witch's castle, and Dorothy is captured.

Dorothy's friends, the Lion, the Scarecrow, and the Tinman regroup and come up with a plan to rescue her.

The Wicked Witch tells Dorothy she will kill her when the hourglass runs out. Dorothy is alone and frightened. She wishes she were home.

Toto escapes and leads the friends to Dorothy to save her.

ACT 3

A New Plan

The protagonist forms a new plan to reach the story goal, energized by the latest info or energy from the Turning Point. The "team" assembles (friends or helpers), and everyone prepares for the final showdown or effort to reach the story goal.

Climax

This is the big moment of the whole story. It is what the action has been building toward. The protagonist and team give their all to reach their goal and defeat any antagonists.

Resolution

After the Climax, this is a period of resolving unfinished parts to your story and showing the protagonist living life in the new world after the antagonist has been defeated.

They try to escape the castle, but the Wicked Witch and her henchmen are right on their trail.

They are trapped, and the Wicked Witch uses her broom to light the Scarecrow on fire. Dorothy splashes him with a pail of water to save him but accidentally splashes the Witch as well. She melts, and her henchmen are happy to be rid of her and give the broom to Dorothy.

Dorothy and her friends triumphantly return to the Emerald City. Dorothy realizes she always had the power to go home with the ruby slippers. She wakes up back in her bed, surrounded by friends and family, happy to be home.

WATCH OUT!

REMEMBER, when you plot, you don't have to write down everything that will happen in your book. As you can see from my example plot sheets, a lot of the story was left out. There is no mention of Munchkins (my favorite part), the fact the Wizard is really a shy inventor, or even anything about the subplots of Dorothy's friends to get a brain, a heart, and courage.

1. Create Your Plot Worksheet

AS YOU FILL OUT your plot worksheet, think about the main story moments that change or shift the story's direction. What would the key elements be if you had to boil your story down? This is what belongs in your plot worksheet. You may want to use a pencil to make changes to it later. If you don't have moments in your story that fit these moments, this is a great time to brainstorm what some of those plot points might look like.

Opening

Here we introduce the protagonist or main character and give the readers a feel for what kind of story it will be and offer a "hook." The hook is some interesting or intriguing scene that will catch the readers, like a fish on a hook, so they won't want to put the book down.

Setup

This section introduces the world's other important characters (such as friends or enemies) and hints at the conflict.

Inciting Incident

This event launches the main events of the story. It comes as a surprise to the protagonist and could be a new problem or opportunity.

Call to Action

After the Inciting Incident, the protagonist must react to the new reality. What will the character do as a result of the Inciting Incident? What is their story goal, or the main thing they now want?

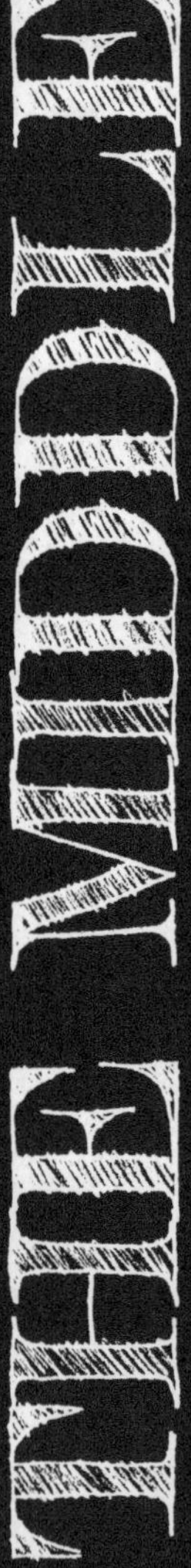

ACT 2
PART ONE

THE MIDDLE

The Choice

The protagonist makes active choices as they move forward, trying to reach their story goal.

Try/Fail

The protagonist and friends/sidekicks try to solve their problems. They fail a lot but have some successes as they move toward the story goal.

Midpoint/Reversal

Some unexpected revelation sends the story in a new direction, raising the stakes. For the first time in the story, the protagonist may doubt if they can do this.

Attack and Bad Guys Regroup

The protagonist tries to carry on, but the bad guys now see them as a serious threat and ramp up their attacks.

Dark Moment

Things are the worst they've ever been. The protagonist loses hope and nearly gives up. There seems to be no way forward.

Turning Point

Something offers hope (a new idea, lucky break, an unseen friend comes through). The protagonist decides to keep going.

ACT 3

A New Plan

The protagonist forms a new plan to reach the story goal, energized by the latest info or energy from the Turning Point. The "team" assembles (friends or helpers), and everyone prepares for the final showdown or effort to reach the story goal.

Climax

This is the big moment of the whole story. It is what the action has been building toward. The protagonist and team give their all to reach their goal and defeat any antagonists.

Resolution

After the Climax, this is a period of resolving unfinished parts to your story and showing the protagonist living life in the new world after the antagonist has been defeated.

STEP 7
DIVIDE YOUR PLOT INTO CHAPTERS

AS WE JUST LEARNED, most stories are broken up into acts. Chapters and scenes occur within each act and help divide the story into manageable sections.

The good news is, by plotting out your novel with the worksheet, you have already broken up your story into acts. Now, let's take a look at chapters.

Most plot points will fall within one chapter, maybe two. You will also have other chapters that fall between these plot points. But plot points aren't your whole story! You are free to develop the story and create chapters that flesh out the sections of the plot, such as try/fail adventures and other fun scenes.

1. Study a Chapter

READ A CHAPTER of your favorite book and answer the following questions.

Title: ____

How many scenes happen within the chapter? (Remember, a new scene is anytime the location, time, or point-of-view changes.)

How did the author let you know the scene was changing?

____

____

Did you feel confused? _______________________________

What kinds of words did the author use to tell you where or when the new scene took place?

_______________________   _______________________

_______________________   _______________________

_______________________   _______________________

Did you learn this in the scene's ☐ beginning, ☐ middle, or ☐ end?

Why do you think the author did this?

____

____

2. Take a Look at Chapter Beginnings

TAKE A BOOK YOU LOVE and just read the first paragraph of each chapter. What phrases does the author use to help the reader understand the chapter's setting/time/point of view? Make a list below of all the phrases you can find, such as "The next morning…" or "Back at the lair…."

__________________________________   __________________________________

__________________________________   __________________________________

__________________________________   __________________________________

__________________________________   __________________________________

__________________________________   __________________________________

__________________________________   __________________________________

__________________________________   __________________________________

__________________________________   __________________________________

__________________________________   __________________________________

Now take a look at the openings of any chapters you've started writing. Have you included any phrases to help your readers transition to your new chapter? Are there any phrases from your list that might work in your book? If so, add them in!

AT THIS POINT, you might be wondering how long to make your book, or maybe how much of your book should be in Act 1, 2, or 3? In the writing world, we use word counts instead of page counts. If you would like to write a typical length novel for your age group, you can shoot for 40,000 words.

But how should those 40,000 words be divided? Ideally, your 1st act should be about 25% of your total book. This is the same for your 3rd act (25%). That means, math drum roll please, your 2nd act should be 50% of your book.

3. Create a Chapter Outline

LOOK AT YOUR one-page story and your plot worksheet and create a chapter outline for your novel on page 92. Make a list of chapters under each Act and one or two sentences about what will happen in that chapter. It doesn't have to be perfect! This list will probably change as you write your book, but it will give you something to work with.

Scenes are mini-stories that link together to make your book.
Like the book itself, each scene needs a beginning, middle, and end.

→ Act 2 is the biggest part of your book and is divided into two parts. Together, all of Act 2 makes up 50% of your book, or 20 chapters.

ACT 2 PART TWO

Right After the Middle

The villain almost crushes the hero, who starts to lose hope. But wait...

Divide 10 chapters between these 3 elements

Attack & Bad Guys Regroup

Dark Moment

Turning Point

ACT 3

End

The hero comes up with a plan that turns things around. And...VICTORY!

Divide 10 chapters between these 3 elements

A New Plan

Climax

Resolution

Each chapter is about 1000 words

CHAPTER 21 | CHAPTER 22 | CHAPTER 23 | CHAPTER 24 | CHAPTER 25 | CHAPTER 26 | CHAPTER 27 | CHAPTER 28 | CHAPTER 29 | CHAPTER 30

Break up each chapter with 1 to 3 scenes

Each chapter is about 1000 words

CHAPTER 31 | CHAPTER 32 | CHAPTER 33 | CHAPTER 34 | CHAPTER 35 | CHAPTER 36 | CHAPTER 37 | CHAPTER 38 | CHAPTER 39 | CHAPTER 40

Break up each chapter with 1 to 3 scenes

This way of breaking down your novel is just a guide. You can have as many (or as few!) chapters and words as you want.

ACT 1

Opening

Introduce the protagonist (and possibly some of the other characters) and give a feel for the kind of story it will be.

Setup

Introduce the other characters (such as friends or enemies) and hint at the conflict.

Inciting Incident

This event launches the main events of the story.

Call to Action

How does the protagonist react to the Inciting Incident?

The Choice

The protagonist makes active choices as they move forward, trying to reach their story goal.

Try/Fail

The protagonist and friends try to solve their problems. They fail but also have some successes as they move toward the story goal.

Midpoint/Reversal

Some unexpected revelation sends the story in a new direction, raising the stakes. For the first time in the story, the protagonist may doubt if they can do this.

Notes

ACT 2 • Part 2

Attack & Bad Guys Regroup

The protagonist tries to carry on but the bad guys now see them as a serious threat and ramp up their attacks.

Dark Moment

Things are the worst they've ever been. The protagonist loses hope and nearly gives up. There seems to be no way forward.

Turning Point

Something offers hope (a new idea, lucky break, an unseen friend comes through). The protagonist decides to keep going.

Notes

ACT 3

A New Plan

The protagonist forms a new plan to reach the story goal, energized by the latest info or energy from the Turning Point.

Climax

The protagonist and team give their all to reach their goal and defeat any antagonists.

Resolution

After the Climax, this is a period of resolving unfinished parts to your story and showing the protagonist living in a "new normal."

Notes

Divide your chapters into scenes

USUALLY, CHAPTERS ARE BROKEN UP into scenes, maybe two or three. Anytime the story (within a chapter) goes to a new location, place in time, or changes point of view, there is usually a new scene. Books typically show scene changes by jumping down two lines and starting a new paragraph. Regular paragraphs only jump down 1 line.

Several scenes might occur in one chapter if we were putting in scene breaks in *The Wizard of Oz.* The chapter might start at the farm, then change scenes as Dorothy goes to see the traveling psychic, then change scenes again as she goes back home—all within the first chapter.

You may be wondering at which point a scene should end? A scene should end when all the necessary action has been accomplished (such as Dorothy realizing she should return home). Another reason it should end is when the conflict/problems are resolved (such as Dorothy melting the Wicked Witch and escaping unharmed).

When should a chapter end? If you've resolved one mini-problem and are heading into a new section of your story, that may be an excellent place to end your chapter. You can also look at the word count and try to keep each of your chapters roughly 1,000 words long. One typed page is around 200 words.

SWITCHING TO A NEW SCENE OR BEGINNING A NEW CHAPTER can confuse your readers if you don't handle it well. These transitions, moments when you are changing to a new scene or chapter, are important not just for clarity but also to make sure you don't lose readers along the way. Chapter endings are a natural place for readers to put down the book to take a break, go to sleep, etc. This is a dangerous moment for a writer! We want to make sure that our readers will come back and won't just decide to put down the book forever.

So, how do we ensure our readers will come back? Easy. Make sure your transitions, your breaks from one chapter to another, are exciting places to end. Hint at the mysteries yet to be revealed. Give your readers a little teaser about the next chapter and what they can look forward to.

4. Add Scenes to Your Chapter Outline

GO BACK TO YOUR CHAPTER OUTLINE. Do you have any ideas what scenes might happen within each chapter? If so, jot these down. If not, no worries! Often scene ideas happen as you're writing.

5. Write a Scene

NOW IT'S TIME TO START WRITING! You can write scenes in this section or go straight to your notebook or computer. You can start at the beginning of your book or write another scene you are excited about. Check them off on your chapter/scene outline as you write them. If you need help with details, check out the References section on page 193.

STEP 8
SET UP SOME ACTION

ACTION IN A STORY is less about car chases and thrilling scenes than about conflict and tension. Conflict is when two or more characters, or forces, want different and opposing things. What does that mean? It means for one to win, one must lose. Conflict keeps your story interesting. If Dorothy arrived in Oz and was able to go on her merry way to the Wizard, skipping and singing with the Munchkins the whole time, the story would be pretty dull. We want there to be something at stake! We want our hero to overcome challenges. This is what we love about stories.

Conflict in a story makes us care and feel invested in what happens. There is something that might be lost, and we find ourselves rooting for the main character and hoping they win. In *The Wizard of Oz*, Dorothy can't just go straight to the Wizard because what she wants—to keep the ruby slippers and get home safely—is precisely the opposite of what the Wicked Witch wants. Someone is opposing her and standing in her way, trying to stop Dorothy from reaching her goal. This is what creates conflict and tension. We suddenly feel the tension that Dorothy must defeat the Witch, or all is lost.

The conflict and action in your plot should intensify, or get stronger, as the story moves along. Each new problem the characters face should build off the problem before it.

ONE MORE THOUGHT about the action of your book. Keeping your story moving has a lot to do with chapter transitions. Ending a chapter on a cliffhanger or at a section where something is hanging in the balance is a great idea. When your readers can't wait to see what happens next, it ensures they will return to the book as soon as possible.

ANOTHER TRICK is to end your chapter in an exciting spot where something has just been revealed. Readers will want to know how the characters will react to the new information and be eager to read on.

1. Finding Your Story's Conflict

LOOK AT YOUR PLOT WORKSHEET and one-page version of your story. Underline in red everywhere you find conflict. Remember, conflict means two or more characters wanting the same thing or opposing each other somehow. Conflict can also come from forces in your book, such as a thick forest the characters must get through, a snowstorm keeping them from reaching their goal, etc. Conflict doesn't just have to come from other characters.

Once you have found your conflict, ask yourself these questions:

☞ **Do you have enough conflict in your story? Does it happen throughout or just in one or two spots? If so, where can you add conflict to keep things exciting?**

☞ **Is your conflict believable? Is there a reason why someone or something is standing in the way of your character and their goals?**

☞ **Is there a way you can increase the tension? How can you make things even harder for your characters and put more at stake?**

2. Insert a "Time Bomb"

A GREAT TIP TO RAMP UP THE CONFLICT and tension in your story is to insert a "time bomb." This means creating some reason your characters can't take forever to solve their problems. By doing this, you force things in your story to happen quickly and raise the stakes. If nothing is at stake—no one will lose anything or gain anything by what is happening—a story isn't interesting. You don't have to create life or death stakes, like with a literal time bomb, but there needs to be fallout or some dire consequence if your characters do not reach their goal. If you have high stakes, plus a time-crunch, you guarantee your story will never be boring.

How can you raise the stakes for your characters? What will happen if your character doesn't get what they want in the story? Can you find a way to make this even worse for them? Is there any place you can insert a "time bomb" and force your characters to act quickly?

3. Writing Your Chapter Endings with Cliffhangers

AS YOU WRITE YOUR FIRST CHAPTERS, look for ways to end your
chapters with a cliffhanger. Can you complete the chapter a little earlier
or maybe a little later? Look for places to end where the story is still in the
middle of an exciting section. Brainstorm some ideas for chapter endings.

4. Take a look at chapter endings

GET OUT A BOOK YOU LOVE.

Title:

Just read the last paragraph or two of each chapter ending.

How many chapters are in the book?

How many of the chapters end with cliffhangers of some kind or another?

Do they reveal some new emotional information?

Yes   No

Do they leave a character in a dangerous situation?

Yes   No

Do they set up any mini-mysteries that you can't wait to solve?

Yes   No

Take notes of techniques the author uses to keep you interested and wanting to read more. How can you incorporate some of these techniques into your chapter endings?

Creating Subplots

ALL SUBPLOTS, or smaller side stories, should help *develop* the main story and grow out of it. Sometimes new writers create subplots by slapping a completely different story onto their first story. Ideally, a subplot should help make your main story richer and more enjoyable. A good subplot might help develop another side of your main character or a side character.

This is not the case with slapped-on subplots. These are minor storylines that are tacked on to the story but don't help develop it. If we took them away, we probably wouldn't even notice.

Think of the subplots in *The Wizard of Oz*. The main story is obviously about Dorothy and her journey to find her way back home or find where she truly belongs. Initially, she doesn't think it is home but learns through her journey that home is where she belongs. The subplots in the story are the friends Dorothy meets along the way and learns to help and care about—the Tin Woodsman, the Cowardly Lion, and the Scarecrow. Each of these side characters has their reason (or story) to join Dorothy on her journey. If you took these subplots away, it doesn't make a lot of sense why they would tag along with her.

The point is to make sure your subplots grow out of your story naturally and become an integral part of it.

BE CAREFUL OF SUBPLOTS springing up all over the place! As your creativity gets going, it is easy to go into overdrive. One or two subplots are plenty. But what if you love all your subplot ideas? It can be painful but don't be afraid to make cuts. You can save the things you cut for another project someday. And nobody wants to read a book trying to drag fifteen subplots along with it. Remember, your main plot is the story, not the subplots.

5.
Discovering Your Subplots

TAKE A LOOK at the plot worksheet you filled out. Do you see any subplots trying to peek out from your story? Are there any places you can develop your characters and their motivations better? If you're having trouble finding subplots, think about *why* your character wants what they want. Is there another story hiding beneath the main one? What about your side characters? What do they want, and why are they on the story journey? Take five minutes to brainstorm three or four side stories you can tell throughout your novel. Once you have done that, narrow it down to your favorite one or two.

6. Don't Forget the Bad/Evil Characters

WHAT ABOUT your antagonist and bad characters? What are their motivations? A subplot can also be why your antagonist is bad to begin with or why they have a grudge or problem with your main character. As you think and play with your story, don't be surprised if mini-stories blossom, all fighting for a chance to have their moment in the sun! Brainstorm all the potential subplots you can create for your main villain, then pick your favorite one and see where pieces of that storyline might fit within your larger story and plot.

STEP 9
WRITE GREAT DIALOGUE

DIALOGUE, OR THE PARTS OF THE BOOK where the characters talk, should sound natural. What does that mean? It means your characters should speak in a way that makes sense for their character. Don't have a little girl sound like a pirate unless that is her particular quirk.

TIPS TO KNOW

THE GOLDEN RULE for dialogue is this: make sure it isn't confusing. Suppose you have a conversation between a lion tamer and a grandma. In that case, we need to know who is talking so we don't accidentally think Grandma is giving us lion-taming tricks and the lion tamer is telling us how to make biscuits. This is why we have dialogue tags like *he said*, *she said*.

YOUR READERS WANT to know who is saying what, but they don't want a bunch of extra info that feels clunky to read. If you have too many dialogue tags, it slows everything down and feels unnatural. You never want to pull the reader out of your story.

WATCH OUT!

Action Beats

ONE WAY TO CLARIFY who is speaking, but avoid too many dialogue tags, is to use action beats. Just like you don't want banana pudding every day of your life, having a big section of *he said, she said, he said, she said,* gets old quickly. Action beats break up the monotony.

Action beats are short sentences that describe the character doing something or thinking something (emotion beats). Look at this example, first without action beats and then with them:

Version 1

"I don't want to go to the fair," Jenny said.

"You have to!" said Randy. "Everybody will be there."

"But I hate clowns," said Jenny.

"It's not that big a deal," said Randy.

Version 2

Jenny marched over to Randy. "I don't want to go to the fair."

"You have to!" said Randy. "Everybody will be there."

"But I hate clowns."

Randy rolled his eyes. "It's not that big a deal."

By including action beats in the second version, we only had to have one *said*. The action beats also gave us a better idea of what each character was thinking and feeling. Now we know Jenny is determined to tell Randy something because she "marched over" to him. We also know that Randy is frustrated by her fear because he "rolled his eyes."

Notice that the third line of dialogue didn't have either an action beat *or* a dialogue tag. With only two people talking, we didn't need it. Most conversations go back and forth, so we are reasonably sure Jenny is speaking. Remember, if you can get away with cutting out a dialogue tag or action beat and it still makes sense who is speaking—do it.

DON'T GO OVERBOARD with your new skill of action beats. Action beats are generally longer than dialogue tags, so they will take up more space and slow your pacing down. No one wants to read fifty descriptive sentences to get through one conversation in your book! So, use them wisely and alternate with dialogue tags. Also, just like anything in your book, an action beat should serve a purpose. Use it to tell us more about the characters, setting, or other info that helps build your world.

Dialogue Guidelines

1. Jump to a new line with every speaker

Every time a new character speaks, jump to a new line. Jay speaks, new paragraph. Bob speaks, new paragraph. Jay speaks again, new paragraph.

2. When using dialogue tags, stick with "said"as much as possible.

You can throw in the occasional *answered, whispered, or yelled*, but generally, stick with *said*. It keeps things simple and is what readers and editors expect.

3. Quotation marks go around speech only (what is being said)

WRONG:

 Bring back my purse! Mary said, as she ran after the thief.

WRONG:

 "Bring back my purse!" Mary said, "as she ran after the thief."

CORRECT

 "Bring back my purse!" Mary said, as she ran after the thief.

We don't put the quotation marks around "as she ran after the thief" because that is an action beat, and Mary isn't saying those words.

4. Punctuation goes inside of quotation marks

Punctuation refers to periods, commas, question marks, exclamation marks. All of these go inside of the quotation marks in the sentence.

WRONG:

 "Help"! Junie said. "My rabbit is lost".

CORRECT:

 "Help!" Junie said. "My rabbit is lost."

The quotation marks give a little hug to the sentence being spoken. Part of that sentence is the exclamation mark and the period. Make sure the punctuation marks get the hug, too, and aren't left out in the cold.

5. Sometimes periods need to be commas

That's right! If your dialogue sentence—the part being spoken—ends with a period AND is followed by a dialogue tag, you leave out the period and put a comma instead. This sounds confusing, but it would look like this:

 "The dance starts at six," said the principal.

Because that sentence ends with a period—it doesn't end in an exclamation point or a question mark—AND has a dialogue tag after it—*said the principal*—we *replace* the period with a comma.

Here is a simple formula to remember:

Period + dialogue tag = change period to comma

WRONG:

 "The dance starts at six." Said the principal.

CORRECT:

 "The dance starts at six," said the principal.

Notice how "said" is NOT capitalized. A dialogue tag following a sentence is NEVER capitalized, even if we use other punctuation.

CORRECT:

 "For the third time, the dance starts at six!" said the irritated principal.

(Still a small "s" for said)

 "The dance starts at six, right?" said the student.

6. Write your speech sentence the same, even if interrupted by action or a dialogue tag

Sometimes, you may choose to break up a character's speech by action or a dialogue tag.

CORRECT:

 "Marty, come back here!" Mom said. "Your homework isn't done."

Since Mom is saying two separate sentences, there is a period after said.

INCORRECT:

 "Marty, come back here!" Mom said, "your homework isn't done."

How do I know this isn't correct? If I took out the dialogue tag, it would look like this:

 "Marty, come back here! your homework isn't done."

See? The word *your* should be capitalized because this is two separate sentences. And since the first sentence is complete, there shouldn't be a comma after "Mom said."

What about one long sentence broken up with action or dialogue tags?

CORRECT:

✔ "Okay, the thing is," Angela said, pacing the room, "we need to find the map to the treasure before the pirates do."

Here I've included both a dialogue tag (Angela said) and an action (pacing the room). Because this is one long sentence, the dialogue tag and action are set off by commas and not periods. When the second part of the sentence picks up again, we DON'T capitalize the first letter because this is still the same sentence.

TIPS TO KNOW

WRITE THE SENTENCE as you typically would. Don't add in extra capitalizations or periods just because you are inserting a dialogue tag or action into the middle of it.

1. Punctuate It Up!

LOOK AT THE FOLLOWING dialogue excerpts. See if you can fill in the blanks and add proper punctuation, such as periods, question marks, etc. Using a red pen will help you see the corrections you make. After you complete them, check your answers on the next page.

Here's a tip: You might need a period if the word after the space is capitalized. If it isn't, you might need a comma.

Dialogue Exercise 1 – Punctuation

Excerpt from *Alice in Wonderland* by Lewis Carroll

"What do you mean by that__" said the Caterpillar sternly__ "Explain yourself__"

"I can't explain myself, I'm afraid, sir__" said Alice__ "because I'm not myself, you see__"

"I don't see__" said the Caterpillar__

"I'm afraid I can't put it more clearly__" Alice replied very politely__ "for I can't understand it myself to begin with, and being so many different sizes in a day is very confusing__"

Answers

Dialogue Exercise 1 - Punctuation

The missing punctuation is in bold.

"What do you mean by that**?**" said the Caterpillar sternly. "Explain yourself**!**"(This could also be a period.)

"I can't explain myself, I'm afraid, sir**,**" said Alice**,** "because I'm not myself, you see**.**"

"I don't see**,**" said the Caterpillar**.**

"I'm afraid I can't put it more clearly**,**" Alice replied very politely, "for I can't understand it myself to begin with, and being so many different sizes in a day is very confusing**.**"

Dialogue Exercise 2 – Punctuation

Excerpt from *The Flying Girl* by L. Frank Baum (writing as Edith Van Dyne)

"Good__" exclaimed Mr. Cumberford__"Then our greatest need is to secure a competent aviator_"

"To operate Stephen's machine_"

"Of course. He's out of commission, poor lad, but the machine must fly, nevertheless__"

Orissa's blue eyes regarded him gravely. She had been considering this proposition ever since the accident.

"Our first task__" said she__ "is to get my brother's invention thoroughly repaired__"

"But the question of the aviator is fully as important__" persisted her friend. "Wilson__" turning to the mechanic__ "do you think you could operate the aircraft__"

Answers

Dialogue Exercise 2 – Punctuation

The missing punctuation is in bold.

"Good**!**" exclaimed Mr. Cumberford**.** "Then our greatest need is to secure a competent aviator**.**"

"To operate Stephen's machine**?**"

"Of course. He's out of commission, poor lad, but the machine must fly, nevertheless**.**"

Orissa's blue eyes regarded him gravely. She had been considering this proposition ever since the accident.

"Our first task," said she**,** "is to get my brother's invention thoroughly repaired**.**"

"But the question of the aviator is fully as important**,**" persisted her friend. "Wilson**,**" turning to the mechanic**,** "do you think you could operate the aircraft**?**"

Dialogue Exercise 3 – Punctuation

Add in the missing punctuation. To make it harder, we've left out the underlines.

Excerpt from *The Wind in the Willows* by Kenneth Grahame

So it is, so it is said the Mole, with great heartiness.

No, it isn't cried the Rat indignantly.

Well then, it isn't replied the Mole soothingly But what I wanted to ask you was, won't you take me to call on Mr. Toad? I've heard so much about him, and I do so want to make his acquaintance

Why, certainly said the good-natured Rat, jumping to his feet and dismissing poetry from his mind for the day Get the boat out, and we'll paddle up there at once. It's never the wrong time to call on Toad. Early or late he's always the same fellow. Always good-tempered, always glad to see you, always sorry when you go

He must be a very nice animal observed the Mole, as he got into the boat and took the sculls, while the Rat settled himself comfortably in the stern.

He is indeed the best of animals replied Rat So simple, so good-natured, and so affectionate. Perhaps he's not very clever—we can't all be geniuses; and it may be that he is both boastful and conceited. But he has got some great qualities, has Toady

Answers

Dialogue Exercise 3 – Punctuation

The missing punctuation is in bold.

"So it is, so it is," said the Mole, with great heartiness.

"No, it isn't!" cried the Rat indignantly.

"Well then, it isn't," replied the Mole soothingly. "But what I wanted to ask you was, won't you take me to call on Mr. Toad? I've heard so much about him, and I do so want to make his acquaintance."

"Why, certainly," said the good-natured Rat, jumping to his feet and dismissing poetry from his mind for the day. "Get the boat out, and we'll paddle up there at once. It's never the wrong time to call on Toad. Early or late he's always the same fellow. Always good-tempered, always glad to see you, always sorry when you go!"

"He must be a very nice animal," observed the Mole, as he got into the boat and took the sculls, while the Rat settled himself comfortably in the stern.

"He is indeed the best of animals," replied Rat. "So simple, so good-natured, and so affectionate. Perhaps he's not very clever—we can't all be geniuses; and it may be that he is both boastful and conceited. But he has got some great qualities, has Toady."

2. Create Dialogue

LOOK AT THE FOLLOWING text and change it from narrative description (telling what happened) to dialogue.

Dialogue Exercise 4 – Creating

Jimmy saw Rajeev and called him over. He asked who had won the basketball game. Rajeev told Jimmy the results and how the Panthers clobbered his team. A few Panthers strolled by and yelled what would happen the next time they played Rajeev's team, the Turkeys. Jimmy shook his head and said maybe Rajeev should consider suggesting a new name for their team. Rajeev smiled and agreed. It was hard to beat anyone when your team was called the Turkeys.

Answers

Dialogue Exercise 4 – Creating

Written as dialogue (your version will be different, but that's okay):

"Hey, Rajeev!" Jimmy called across the parking lot.

Rajeev jogged over in his basketball uniform.

Jimmy high-fived him. "So, who won the game?"

Rajeev deflated. "Aww, man! The Panthers, of course. They clobbered us."

The gym door opened, and three players from the Panthers's team strolled out.

"Hey, look! It's one of those Turkeys," a tall boy yelled. "Next time, we won't go easy on you! Next time, it'll be a fifty-point lead!"

The two other boys laughed as they got on the bus.

Jimmy shook his head. "You know, Rajeev, I'm a big fan of your team. But maybe you guys should consider a new name?"

Rajeev smiled. "Yeah, I guess you're right. It's hard to beat anyone when your team is called the Turkeys."

3. Format for Dialogue

FORMAT THE FOLLOWING short paragraph into the correct formatting for dialogue (with quotation marks, punctuation, and paragraph breaks)

Dialogue Exercise 5 - Formatting

Come here, Sally Roger almost tripped over a rock in his yard as he ran after his dog What's wrong called a man walking a short wiener dog My dog got loose again and she won't listen to me The man nodded, then reached down and slipped the leash off his dog Kaiser Go he said The squat dog took off toward the bushes Roger waited anxiously Wouldn't this just get *two* dogs lost Gee, I'm not sure you should have But he didn't get to finish There was Sally following obediently behind Kaiser, like a little soldier Roger ran up and grabbed her leash Thank you so much he said The man just nodded, slipped the leash back onto Kaiser, and continued on his walk Sally panted up at Roger Come on, let's go on a walk. But this time, you're staying with me

Answers

Dialogue Exercise 5 – Formatting

"Come here, Sally!" Roger almost tripped over a rock in his yard as he ran after his dog.

"What's wrong?" called a man walking a short wiener dog.

"My dog got loose again and she won't listen to me."

The man nodded, then reached down and slipped the leash off his dog. "Kaiser, go!" he said.

The squat dog took off toward the bushes.

Roger waited anxiously. Wouldn't this just get *two* dogs lost? "Gee, I'm not sure you should have…" but he didn't get to finish.

There was Sally following obediently behind Kaiser, like a little soldier.

Roger ran up and grabbed her leash. "Thank you so much," he said.

The man just nodded, slipped the leash back onto Kaiser, and continued on his walk.

Sally panted up at Roger.

"Come on, let's go on a walk. But this time, you're staying with me!"

Note: The line "Wouldn't this just get two dogs lost?" should not be in quotes because this is Roger's thought, not something spoken out loud. Also, you can use an ellipsis (…) to signify speech that is trailing off and not finished.

4. Study Dialogue

TAKE OUT ONE of your favorite books.

Title: Page:

Skim ahead until you find a section of dialogue.

How many times does the author use the word *said*?

How many action beats occur?

Does the author often leave out dialogue tags and action beats altogether?

Do you notice a pattern in the way the author uses or doesn't use dialogue tags?

Does the author use other words besides *said*? If so, what are they?

What have you learned that you can use in your own writing?

STEP 10
BUILD TO THE CLIMAX

TIPS TO KNOW

THE MOMENT when everything comes to a head is called the climax. It's the point in the story that will decide the fate of everything. If this part of the story is good, we tell all our friends we just read a great book! If this part of the story is terrible, we chuck the book across the room and feel cheated. So, how do you write a good climax that will not disappoint your readers? Take a look at the exercises on the next page.

MAKE SURE YOUR CLIMAX FITS with the rest of your story. Climaxes aren't just chase scenes and explosions. Don't think you need to add these into your story about three little old ladies who drink tea and talk about life.

WATCH OUT!

1. Ramp Up the External Conflict

EXTERNAL CONFLICT means all the things that are happening outwardly in the story, not inside a character (such as their feelings). As you move toward the story's climax, everything should get bigger, faster, and more intense.

Look at your plot worksheet.

☞ **Can you insert a "time bomb?"**

☞ **Can you make something else happen to cut your already shortened time in half again?**

☞ **What tricks can your villain suddenly pull out at the last minute to make things harder for your characters?**

Brainstorm how you can increase the tension and conflict in this last push of your story.

2. Ramp Up the Internal Conflict

THE INTERNAL CONFLICT refers to the forces inside your character that pull them in opposite directions. It is their split allegiances, their guilt, their desire to help themselves but also help their friends. It may be the pull to seize what they want or to do the right thing. Often villains play with our character's internal conflict as they try to tempt them to give up, join them, or make some other devious suggestion.

Increasing internal conflict is especially important in "quieter" stories, where there are no car chases, moments of mortal peril, etc. Look at your plot worksheet.

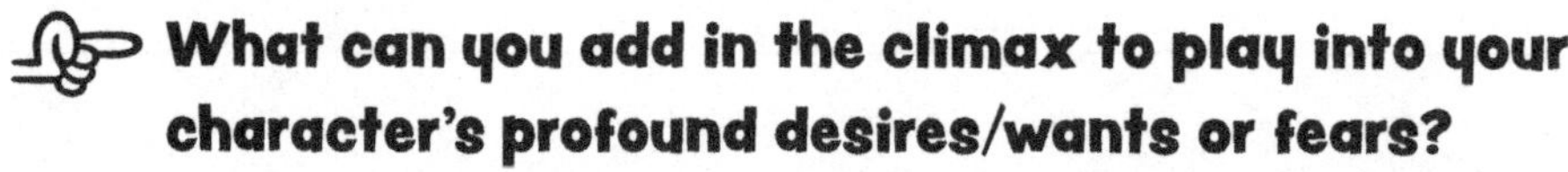 **What can you add in the climax to play into your character's profound desires/wants or fears?**

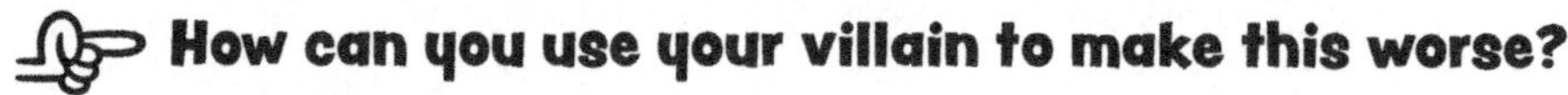 **How can you use your villain to make this worse?**

This is not the time to be nice! Throw everything you can at them and help them be victorious anyway. Your readers will love it.

3. Use Setting/Location to Ramp up Intensity

THE CHOICE of where to place your final action can make or break your climax. Use your setting to your advantage for these final climactic scenes. You can set things at the top of a cliff, on the tower of a witch's castle, or a sinking ship. The choice of your location can add or take away from the scene's intensity.

Remember, you have the power to set the stage almost anywhere as long as it makes sense in your story world. Take a look at your plot worksheet.

☞ **Where have you decided to set your climactic scene?**

☞ **How will this setting add the most drama and raise the stakes for your characters?**

4. Structure Your Final Chapters and Scenes to Add to the Tension

REMEMBER, everything should ramp up as your story speeds toward your climax. Your pacing—how quickly the story unfolds—should grow and gain momentum. This is not the time to include those "catch a breath" scenes or have your characters go to the library for research. This is the time to build and keep the tension high until the end of the climax.

One way to do this is to structure your chapters and scenes to increase the tension. Shorter sentences, action, and revelations at every turn are cliff-hangers that keep us involved. Take some notes as you plan out your climax.

☞ **What kind of dramatic or action-packed events can happen in this scene?**

☞ **What kind of cliffhangers or revelations can you spring on your readers?**

FINISHED NOVEL

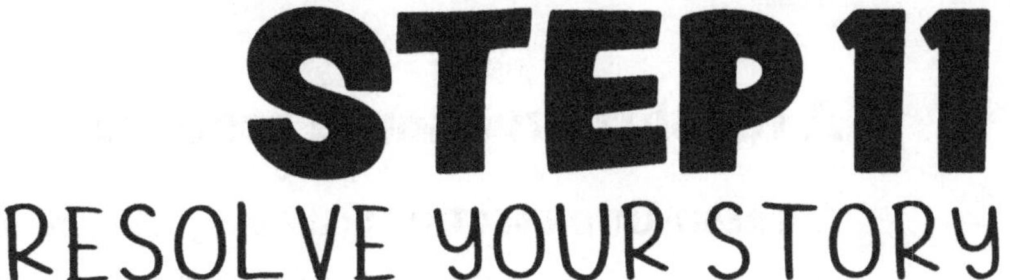

STEP 11
RESOLVE YOUR STORY

THE RESOLUTION OF YOUR STORY comes between the amazing climax of the book and writing *The End*. Why is resolution important? We need to see the characters make it back to some relatively normal life, even if it's a new normal.

In *The Wizard of Oz*, the climax happens when Dorothy throws water on the wicked witch and defeats her once and for all. However, it wouldn't feel right if the story just ended there. What about getting back to Kansas? What about "There's no place like home?"

This is where resolution comes in. We need to *resolve* some things so the story can finish.

A resolution should resolve

THE RESOLUTION SECTION of the story is where you tie all the loose ends up. Have you given a satisfying ending to your central plot line and minor subplots? Have you given a scene to show your characters back in their normal world or their world's "new normal" from their changed perspective?

Create a great ending image

HOPEFULLY, by the end of your novel, your readers will come to know and love your characters as much as you do. Give your readers a chance to slow down and say goodbye. Think about the last feeling you want to leave them with. You want that last impression of your story to leave readers with a good feeling.

IT'S EASY to make your resolution too short. Give enough time to slow the pace down from the hectic go, go, go of the climax. One or two lines, even one paragraph, is not enough for a resolution. I know it is fun to get to the end, but make sure you give your readers adequate time to catch their breath and settle in for this final scene or chapter.

ANOTHER TEMPTATION is to make the resolution too long. What if Dorothy made it back to Kansas, woke up and saw her family and friends, and THEN got out of bed, made some biscuits, took a bath, and started helping Auntie Em with her quilt project. This would leave the audience baffled. Just why hasn't the story ended yet? Don't do that. Get in, resolve the story and loose ends, and get out.

1. Loose Ends

TAKE A LOOK at your plot worksheet on page 76. List out all the major and minor storylines. Do you have ideas for resolving these? Are there any you forgot about? Don't forget your villain as well. Have you created a satisfying ending for all the major characters in your story?

2. Brainstorm your ending

WHERE DOES YOUR STORY BEGIN? How can you bring your story full circle back to where your main character started, but with a new understanding now?

☞ **What kind of feeling would you like your readers to take away with them as they finish up your book?**

☞ **What type of scene might create that feeling?**

GET WRITING

It's time to write your first draft! You've done the hard part by outlining your book—now it's time to fill in all the holes. Use the Character Profiles (page 30) and the Plot Worksheet (page 76) you created, along with all the notes you've made, and start writing!

OP
Before moving on, it's time
to finish your first draft!

Before you move on to Step 12, take your draft and put it in a drawer for at least a week and forget about it! A month is even better, but if you're anxious to get back to it, a week will do.

By not thinking about your novel for a while, you'll come back to it with fresh eyes, and that's what you need for Step 12—Revise and Edit.

STEP 12
REVISE AND EDIT

CONGRATULATIONS! If you are at this point, you have finished writing your novel. That's amazing! You are now ready to begin a new stage—editing your book. It's important to remember books are written in stages. You have just finished a first draft, or version, of your story. I suggest you set the whole thing aside for at least a week, preferably more. Taking a break from your writing will help you come back to it with a fresh perspective and find what needs to be improved or changed.

Sometimes writers feel sad when they realize their novel isn't done or "good enough" yet to publish. But do you know who else's first draft wasn't as good as they hoped? Only EVERY WRITER WHO EVER LIVED! Seriously! Shakespeare? He revised. J.K. Rowling? Also, a reviser. Almost every author you love? You guessed it! They revised and edited their stories until they were done.

So, how do you edit your book? What should you be looking for as you read it? We go into all that right here!

JUST BECAUSE your book isn't perfect after the first draft doesn't mean it's not going to be good. You just aren't done yet. *Don't compare your first draft with a published book.*

WATCH OUT!

1. Read Your Book

READ YOUR BOOK and takes notes! If you can print your book out, that is helpful. As you read, make notes wherever something is confusing, dull, or seems pointless or no longer relevant to the story you are telling. Sometimes we set out writing one story and then end up with a different one at the end! This is totally fine, but it needs to be fixed. Make a note of everywhere that might need to be changed or cut, such as:

 **Weird subplots that don't tie in.**

Unnecessary characters or scenes.

Dialogue that goes too long and is irrelevant.

Descriptions that stretch on forever.

Also, note other areas where you need more details, such as confusing passages. You may also notice flat characters that need to be better developed.

2. Make Significant Changes (if needed)

DON'T SPEND FOREVER making each word and sentence beautiful when you may end up cutting that whole scene later. This isn't the time for that kind of editing. Right now, you are focusing on the big picture, the structure of your book. This big-picture editing is called doing a *structural* or *developmental edit.* You need to make sure the shape of your story is right, your Acts have the right proportion to each other, and you didn't accidentally write too much in Act 1 and too little in Act 3.

Flip back to your plot worksheet on page 76. Does your draft match it, or did you change a lot? Change is okay, but you need to make a new plot worksheet if you changed a lot to see if you have plot holes and problems with your structure. You may need a whole new beginning or a different middle section. On the other hand, your story might match your plot worksheet pretty closely and may not need any structural changes.

When you're happy with the big picture structure of your story, look at your chapters and see if each one is necessary to the story. Cut anything that isn't necessary to the plot, character development, or if it doesn't add fun to your book. As you make changes, you are creating the second draft of your story.

3. Make Smaller Changes

NOW, YOU'RE READY to begin your third draft. Your big picture structure is pretty good. You've cut a lot of extra fluff and distracting parts. Now get into each chapter, scene, paragraph, and sentence. Again, start big and go down from there. Do you need everything in this chapter? Is this scene necessary? Do you need three paragraphs to describe your character's clothes? (The answer is no). Look at each sentence and cut filler words—*that*, *really*, *seemed*, *very*, *kind of*. Tighten up your descriptions. Pick the best image of what the woods were like, and use that.

Read your book out loud or listen to it played to you through a text-to-speech program. Software like Microsoft Word and Google Docs have text-to-speech capabilities. The computer will read your book to you. Hearing your words aloud is helpful for catching minor mistakes, typos, and clunky sentences.

Read your book and note the places you were bored. Look for ways to shorten or cut those sections or change the wording to make them more interesting.

Make sure your dialogue formatting is correct and flows well. Again, there is no replacement for listening to it out loud. Does it sound like actual speech? If not, re-work it.

4. Practice Editing

EDITING ISN'T AN EXACT SCIENCE. Sure, there are grammar rules, but a lot of editing deals with fixing story problems, finding the best word or way to say something, and helping the writing flow. Like with writing, editing is something you get better at with practice and more practice. The cool thing is, as you grow as a writer, you will also grow as an editor and vice versa.

For these next two exercises, read the scenes and then look for the following to edit:

👉 **Places where the word choice could be better (if any words jump out at you as weird, that's a good clue it needs to be changed).** Try to think of stronger words and verbs for the poor ones. Remember, "stronger" words are often more precise and paint a better picture in your reader's mind.

👉 **Places where there is too much description or boring details. Keep one or two descriptions and cut the rest.**

👉 **Sentences that are too long. Look for ways to break these up into shorter sentences.**

👉 **Filler words (that, very, so, weak verbs). Remove entirely or rework the sentence so they are not needed.**

👉 **Telling. Look for places you can change telling into showing, especially when it's an emotion.**

When you are done editing, check your answers on the following page. Your edits won't be the same as mine, but that's okay—a lot of editing is subjective and each scene will be different from person to person. What we're tying to do is make the scene the best it can be.

Editing Exercise 1

Strike through words with your pen, use arrows to indicate where you want to move sections and write in the spaces between each sentence. Your markups don't have to make sense to anyone but you, and if you're not sure about a change, circle the word or sentence and decide on the edit later.

Braedon beheld the cracked, grey, aging basketball court, avoiding Colin's gaze. He was nervous.

"Don't worry," Colin squeaked, taking a shot. "He's not here."

"Worried about what?" Braedon joked, pretending that his friend didn't know exactly what he was so very perturbed about. Everyone in the seventh grade at McMicken Heights Middle School in Boise, Idaho knew that Luke wanted nothing more than to kill him ever since Braedon had accidentally tripped in

the cafeteria on Tuesday at lunchtime and leaked his
spaghetti-o's all down the front of Luke's green shirt.

Braedon purloined the round, hard, orange
basketball sphere with stripes from Colin, who stood
almost as tall as he did and wore a very blue plaid
shirt with green buttons.

"Hey!" Colin chirped. "No fair." The two amigos
played basketball until a tall, very large boy with
spikey hair walked up to them. He was angry.

Braedon jostled Colin with his elbow, and tried to
hide that he was afraid.

It was Luke!

Answers

Editing Exercise 1

YOUR MARKUPS won't be the same as mine and that's okay. The point of editing is to go over your text looking for ways to make it better. You could give this exercise to 100 different people and each result would be different!

Braedon ~~beheld the cracked, grey,~~ (aging) basketball [*scanned? looked around?* | *leave in?*]

court, avoiding Colin's gaze. He was nervous.

"Don't worry," Colin ~~squeaked~~ *said*, taking a shot. "He's

not here."

"Worr~~ied~~ *worry* about what?" Braedon joked, pretending

that his friend didn't know (exactly) *italics* what he was so

~~very perturbed~~ *worried* about. Everyone in the seventh grade

~~at McMicken Heights Middle School in Boise, Idaho~~

knew ~~that~~ Luke wanted nothing more than to kill

him. ever since ~~Braedon had accidentally~~ tripped in *Luke hated Braedon* / *he* the cafeteria ~~on Tuesday at lunchtime~~ and ~~leaked his~~ **dumped**

capital s spaghetti-o's ~~all~~ down the front of Luke's ~~green~~ shirt.

We don't need "accidentally" because tripping is always accidental and we don't need details about when the accident in the cafeteria was.

Braedon ~~purloined~~ **stole** the ~~round, hard, orange~~ basketball ~~sphere with stripes~~ from Colin, ~~who stood almost as tall as he did and wore a very blue plaid shirt with green buttons.~~

Always choose a simple word like "stole" over an obscure one like "purloined." We don't need any of this description about Colin.

"Hey!" Colin ~~chirped~~ **yelled**. "No fair." The two ~~amigos~~ **friends** played ~~basketball~~ until a ~~tall, very large~~ **huge** boy ~~with~~ ~~spikey hair~~ walked up~~,~~ **, gritting his teeth** ~~to them. He was angry.~~

You can say "yelled" or "said." Get rid of "very" and use a better adjective if possible. Instead of "he was angry," (which is telling), we can show Luke's anger by saying he was "gritting his teeth."

Braedon ~~jostled Colin with his elbow,~~ **elbowed Colin** and ~~tried to~~ **shoved his hands in his pockets to keep them from shaking.** ~~hide that he was afraid.~~

The word "elbowed" turns four words into one and sounds better. Shoving hands into pockets to keep them from shaking shows us that Braedon is scared instead of telling us.

It was Luke!

Editing Exercise 2

I hate winter break! Maybe this makes me very weird? I don't know. I just know that it is so boring being home all day, alone. All I do is watch old tv shows on my laptop. Some kids at Bailey Heights Middle School think it is very cool to be the sole child my mother gave birth to. They say things like, "Hey, you get all the wrapped in paper boxes with bows on them to yourself!"

But being alone in the time of year when it is cold and the snow falls down is the very worst! I feel sad and end up eating all the Oreos from the cupboard that Grandpa painted last year. It used to be orange, but now it's navy blue. Not really navy blue, maybe lighter than that. It took him three

days to paint all the cupboards in the kitchen.

My Mom works at an office where they examine

and clean teeth. She feels worried that I'm bored

at home all day and eating Oreos. But at least the

break isn't forever!

Answers

Editing Exercise 2

When winter break comes, I wish I had a time machine to skip over it. ~~I hate winter break!~~ Maybe this makes me ~~very~~ weird? I don't know. I just know ~~that it is so boring~~ the hours creep by when I'm ~~being~~ home all day, alone. All I do is watch old tv shows on my laptop. Some kids at ~~Bailey Heights~~ school ~~Middle School~~ think ~~it is very~~ it's cool to be ~~the sole~~ ~~child my mother gave birth to~~ an only child. They say things like, "Hey, you get all the ~~wrapped in paper boxes with~~ presents, But Tamika, ~~bows on them~~ to yourself!"

But being alone in ~~the time of year when it is~~ winter ~~cold and the snow falls down~~ is the ~~very~~ worst! I stay in bed way too long and wander around the empty house, ~~feel sad and~~ end up eating all the Oreos. ~~from the cupboard that Grandpa painted last year. It used to be orange, but now it's navy blue. Not really navy~~ then

~~blue, maybe lighter than that. It took him three~~

~~days to paint all the cupboards in the kitchen.~~

a dentist's office
My Mom works at ~~an office where they examine~~

and calls me three times a day to say
~~and clean teeth. She feels worried that I'm bored at~~

"You aren't just moping around
~~home all day and~~ eating Oreos~~.~~, are you?"

But at least the break isn't forever!

5. Get feedback from readers

FIND A FEW PEOPLE you know and trust, such as family and friends. I suggest starting with people you know, preferably people similar to your ideal audience. For example, if your story is an epic fantasy about vampires in the old west, don't have your grandma read it unless she likes monsters and cowboys. Instead, ask a friend who likes the same books you like.

STEP 13
PUBLISH YOUR BOOK

TRADITIONAL PUBLISHING is what most of us mean when we say a book is "published." In this day and age, self-publishing (also called independent publishing) is also a great option.

Traditional publishing

Let's look at this option first. The bulk of the books at your library are traditionally published, as are the books at your school. But you can't just send your manuscript off to a publisher, at least not most of them. To be published traditionally, you need an agent. Literary agents accept submissions from writers who want to get their stories published. If the agent thinks your story is well-developed and has a unique enough idea, and if it is the sort of story they represent, they may choose to take you on as a client. Not all literary agents represent the same kinds of books.

YOU CAN GO TO Manuscriptwishlist.com and find agents who are open to submissions and represent the kind of book you write. Just make sure you follow their submission guidelines exactly! That means if they say to send your sample chapter in 12 pt. Times New Roman font, don't send it in Comic Sans.

UNFORTUNATELY, there are scammers and crooks in the publishing world. Never pay money to a publisher to publish your book. Never pay money to a literary agent to read your book or take you on as a client. Legitimate publishers and agents make money from selling your book, not from authors giving them money!

Traditional publishing

PROS

- you'll have someone walk you through each step
- books will be sold in stores and online

The publishing house takes care of:

- editing
- formatting
- design
- illustration
- book launch
- marketing

CONS

- Each publishing house is looking for certain types of books, and only publishes a handful of them a year.
- You have to find the right publishing house for your type of book by sending numerous query letters.
- If your book is chosen, it could take a year or longer for it to be published.

1. Write a Query Letter

ONCE YOU FIND four or five agents you want to contact, it's time to send a query letter. Querying is the process of sending a one-page introductory letter to an agent which includes a brief pitch for your book. The letter also has a sentence or two about yourself and a comment about why you think *this* book is a right fit for *them*. Your query letter should also include the word count of your project and what genre it falls into. All this can sound confusing, but take a look at these top query letter tips:

1. Keep your whole letter to 1 page, single-spaced, and under 300 words.

2. Follow the proven format for query letters (see example on the next page)

3. In your paragraph about your book, you are NOT trying to summarize your whole book! You ARE trying to tell the hook of your book, which should include what your main character wants, why they want it, and what is keeping them from getting it. The point of this "hook" is to get the agent to request your book for further reading. Do NOT give away the ending!

4. In your bio sentence, keep it brief and only include information about yourself that helps the agent know why you're the best person to write your story. As a young author, you can mention your age if you want, but you don't have to. The cool thing about publishing fiction is that it is all about your book. If your book is well-written and finds the right publisher at the right time, it won't matter if you are 12 or 68.

Your Name
Street Address
City, State, Zip Code
Your Phone Number
Your e-mail Address

Date

Agent's Name
Agent Title
Literary Agency Name
Street Address
City, State, Zip Code

Dear (make sure you find out the agent's name),

This is where you write why you are submitting to this agent. Talk about why you chose to query them. How do you know they represent your kind of book?

This is where you get right into your pitch. Tell the hook of your novel. What makes your story unique and exciting? Who is your main character? What do they want? What is keeping them from what they want?

You can take around two paragraphs for this part of the letter. You don't need to mention any side plots here, and definitely don't give away the ending. This teaser is designed to get the agent to request more of your book and get them interested in reading the whole story. If you struggle to write this section of your query, go to the library and read the short blurbs (sales pitches) that show up on the back or inside some popular books.

Once you have told your hook, state the necessary information about your book right here, including title, word count, and genre/category. Even if you don't have a title you love, come up with something for now. You can always change it later. Here is an example of what you might write in this section: *My novel, Junie and Roger Get Zapped, is a middle school adventure story and is 40,320 words.*

In this final paragraph, write a sentence or two about yourself. If you've received any awards or recognition for writing, add it here.

Thank you for your consideration,

Your Name

Self-publishing

IF SOMEONE HEARD the term "self-published" not that long ago, they would assume your book wasn't good enough to be traditionally published. That is not the case at all! Self-publishing is a legitimate way to become a published author. Many self-published authors have more sales and readers than some traditionally published authors.

With the revolution of print on demand, it doesn't have to cost money upfront to self-publish your book. With print on demand publishers, such as Amazon or IngramSpark, all you need to do is upload your book to their website and make it available to the public. A physical book is printed and shipped out when someone buys your book. You get a percentage of the money from that sale. Ebooks are also available with self-publishing.

If you self-publish, it's crucial to realize YOU are the editor, proofreader, cover designer, marketing expert, and more! You won't have a publisher helping you with any of this. But the plus side is, you can upload your book, order it, and have it show up at your door. You can put it on your shelf and be proud that you wrote your own novel. You can even give it to your grandma as a present. I bet she'd love it!

Self-publishing your book on Amazon

1. Format your book

Before your manuscript can be printed as a book, it needs to be formatted. The simplest way to do this on Amazon is to download the free program **Kindle Create** from Amazon.com. (Make sure to get permission from an adult, first!)

Download the right version for your computer, either PC or Mac. The program will walk you through uploading your book file and help you decide how the inside of your book will look. When you're done, generate a "preview" of your book, both as an eBook and as a paperback, and fix any formatting errors that may arise. Hit the "generate" button and save the file when everything looks good.

2. Create a cover

No matter what the saying is, books are judged by their covers, so make sure you have a good one! Amazon makes it easy to make a cover for your formatted book, or if you'd prefer to have a bit more artistic freedom, there are free book cover design programs online that you can use to create a great cover.

Amazon's tool is called *Cover Creator* and once you upload your formatted book, it will give you the option to use it.

Other FREE book cover design tools to check out include:

Canva
https://www.canva.com/create/book-covers/
(Easy to use; walks you through all the steps)

Visme
https://www.visme.co/book-cover-maker/
(Easy to use; lots of free templates available)

PosterMyWall
https://www.postermywall.com/index.php/sizes/book-cover-template
(Pick from book cover templates and customize. Some free options)

WATCH OUT! **TO NOT VIOLATE** any copyright laws, you have to be the creator of the images you use or have permission to use the images for your cover. If you don't, your book (and you) could get into trouble. But the good news is that any images you get through a cover design tool listed here are free of copyright issues.

3. Create an Amazon KDP (Kindle Direct Publishing) account

With help and permission from an adult, create an account with Amazon KDP. If you already have an Amazon account, you will sign in with that information.

https://kdp.amazon.com/en_US/help/topic/G200620010

You will then put in your author information and set up a way to get paid from your book sales.

4. Enter the book details and upload your book

While logged into Amazon KDP, go to the "Bookshelf" section at the top of the page. Click the "+" button to create a new book under the "Create a New Title" section of the page. Book description, keywords, and categories are critical, and readers will use this information when searching for books to read. There are helpful tips at the link below for how to create these details:

https://kdp.amazon.com/en_US/help/topic/G202172740

You will then be prompted to upload your book. This is where you will upload the formatted file you created in Kindle Create. You will also upload a separate file for your cover. Use the file you created in Cover Create, or in the other book cover software program.

You will get to preview your book, get an ISBN (a unique identification number for books), and set up your book's print options.

Lastly, you will set up your book's price and royalty rate. The price is the amount others will pay to purchase your book. You can adjust this price later as well and change it any time. The royalty rate is the percentage of the price you receive for your book. You don't get 100% of your price because Amazon gets some of the profits for printing and advertising your book on their website. As you make these choices, click on the links provided for helpful tips and guidance in choosing the price and royalties. Before publishing, you and an adult must agree to the terms and conditions of publishing through Amazon.

5. Publish your book!

You did it! It is now time to submit your book for publication. You may also choose to order a proof copy at this time before publishing to see what your book will look like when printed out.

Congratulations! Soon you will be holding your own book in your hands. You should be proud of yourself and what you've accomplished. But don't celebrate too long; your next book is waiting to be written!

Self-publishing

PROS

- You have total control and can publish any book any time you want.
- Upload it to Amazon Kindle Direct Publishing and reach millions of potential readers.

CONS

You have to take care of the following:

- editing
- formatting
- design
- illustration
- book launch
- marketing

- If you can't do all of the above yourself, you'll have to hire someone to help.
- The book is only sold online.
- If you don't market it well, your friends and family may be the only ones to see it.

Congratulations!

If you've followed all the exercises in the book, you're close to having a finished novel—that's further than most people get!

The following chapter shares some additional tips and advice. If you get stuck, you can refer to these pages.

REFERENCES

Show, Don't Tell

IF YOU STAY long in the writing world, eventually someone will tell you, "Show, don't tell." That means try your best to paint pictures with words for your readers to see, rather than just telling them your information.

For instance, we could say,

Jenny was sad.

And you might picture Jenny crying, I might picture her looking out over the ocean, and someone else might see Jenny curled up on her bed. Overall, just telling us "Jenny was sad" is pretty vague and can be painted in a million different ways. It also doesn't particularly make me, as the reader, feel anything.

Now, let's *show* Jenny being sad. I might write,

Jenny picked at the hole on her jeans and bit her lip. A pit grew in her stomach and the words, *Just give me any partner as long as it isn't Jenny*, bounced around inside her.

See the difference? This example *shows* how Jenny felt sad. It uses the sensations she felt, the things she did, and her thoughts. Nowhere did I say "Jenny was sad," but we still know that. We also have more of a clue *why* she's sad as well. This is why showing is so powerful.

However, it's necessary to know you can "tell" things as well. Telling is especially helpful when you need your readers to know something, but you don't want to take the time to show it. For example, I may need the readers to know a scene takes place after school, but I don't want to show leaving school, getting on the school bus, riding home, getting out, and walking the half block to my character's house. Telling takes a lot less time than showing! I can literally just say, "After school…" and move on.

However, new writers often error on the side of too much telling. While you can't possibly *show* everything in your novel, it is helpful to look for places you have *told* something that might be better *shown*.

What would his mouth be doing?
What would his eyes be doing?
What would his hands be doing?
What would his heart be doing?
What would his stomach be doing?
What would his feet be doing?

Showing emotion through body language

FEELINGS AND EMOTIONS are better to *show* than *tell*. Try to pinpoint what your character is feeling. What kinds of sensations happen to you when you feel that emotion? Pay attention to what you, and others, do when you're angry, scared, happy. Try to give your characters physical movements that they do when they feel certain things too.

If you feel stuck, here is a list you can use to show your characters as they experience different emotions.

Anger

Reddened face, hitting things, slamming fists down on the table, gritting teeth, stomping away, tightening shoulders, getting quiet, staring

Sadness

Crying, moaning, curling up, moving slowly, staring off, sobbing, shaking, dragging feet when walking, being silent, biting lip, breathing heavy

Happiness

Smiling, laughing, jumping, running, talking loudly, waving arms around, talking fast, hugging, standing back (taking it all in), tearing up

Boredom

Looking off, fiddling with hands, sliding down in the seat, dragging feet, whining, rolling eyes, sighing

Anxiety/Fear

Sweaty palms, fluttering in stomach, tight stomach, stomach ache, pounding in the chest, not paying attention/easily distracted, crying, shaking, shaking a leg up and down, breathing quickly, running away

Confusion

Shaking head, tilting head, muttering to oneself, shrugging shoulders, frowning, squinting

Embarrassment

Blushing, looking away or down, fidgeting, moving feet, slouching shoulders, trying to hide, slinking down in the seat, covering face with hands, giggling, talking too much

Jealousy

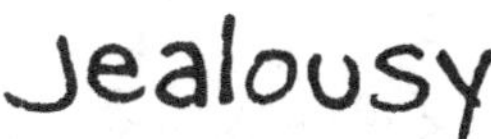

Squinting eyes, frowning, staring hard, burning in the chest

Hiding Something

Avoiding eye contact, changing the subject, looking off, talking too loudly, forcing a smile, hands in pockets or behind back

Annoyance

Biting lips, rolling eyes, looking off for a way to escape, turning body away from annoying thing/person, sighing

What else can you show?

Feelings aren't the only thing to show in your writing. As you paint a picture of the world of your book, including sensory details like sound, sight, smell, taste, touch can help your reader enter into your story world.

Ways to show sounds

Have you ever heard of Onomatopoeia? These words sound like the thing they are describing, such as "beep" or "clink." These words do double duty because they not only describe what something is like or does, but they also lend some musicality to your words.

Ways to show smells

Like with sound, including smells into your writing helps create a world your readers can experience. If I asked you to think of visiting your grandparents, I bet the smells of your grandma cooking traditional foods would come to mind. Have you ever found a toy from your early childhood and smelled it? Nothing like a smell to transport you back through the years!

Antiseptic • Bouquet • Citrusy • Comforting

Coppery • Damp • Delicious • Earthy

Faint • Fetid • Fishy • Floral

Flowery • Fragrant • Fresh • Fruity

Funky • Heavy • Intoxicating • Lemony

Leathery • Medicinal • Minty • Musky

Nasty • Nauseating • Overpowering

Powerful • Pungent • Putrid • Rancid

Rank • Reek • Rich • Ripe

Savoury • Skunky • Smoky

Sour • Stale • Stuffy • Sweet

Tangy • Whiff • Woody

Ways to show touch

Sometimes writers forget about touch. Don't be one of those writers! Describing how something feels to the touch can be a compelling description. What better way to ground your readers in the story world?

Here are 56 words to describe the feel if you get stuck:

Abrasive	Gooey	Oily	Silky
Barbed	Grainy	Padded	Slippery
Bristly	Grimy	Pointy	Soggy
Clammy	Hairy	Pot-holed	Spongy
Cool	Hot	Prickly	Stubbly
Damp	Icy	Ragged	Thick
Doughy	Itchy	Razor-sharp	Thorny
Dusty	Jagged	Rigid	Tough
Embossed	Knitted	Rough	Uneven
Etched	Limp	Sandy	Velvety
Feathery	Lumpy	Scalding	Veneered
Frothy	Malleable	Serrated	Warm
Fuzzy	Moist	Shaggy	Wiry
Gelatinous	Mushy		Wrinkled

More About Action beats and Dialogue Tags

Action beats describe the action of the character who's talking. They share more information about the character than dialogue tags.

DIALOGUE TAGS are simple ways to tell the reader who's speaking:

he/she/they/I said.

she/he/they/I answered.

Pam yelled, or yelled Pam.

Judy asked, or asked Judy.

the mouse whispered, or whispered the mouse.

The tag can come before the dialogue, after, or in the middle:

Pam yelled, "Get out of here, or else!"

"Get out of here, or else!" yelled Pam.

"Get out of here," Pam yelled, "or else!"

ACTION BEATS can be used with dialogue tags and can come before, after, or in the middle of dialogue:

The mouse sniffed the wedge of parmesan and whispered, "Cheese. I love cheese."

"Cheese. I love cheese," whispered the mouse, **sniffing the wedge of parmesan.**

"Cheese," the mouse whispered, **sniffing the wedge of parmesan.** "I love cheese."

Action beats can be used to replace dialogue tags entirely and can come before, after, or in the middle of dialogue:

> **I looked out over the horizon, then at Hank.** "This isn't going to be easy."

> "This isn't going to be easy." **I looked out over the horizon, then at Hank.**

> "This isn't…" **I looked out over the horizon, then at Hank,** "…this isn't going to be easy."

Action beats are used to show characterization, setting, mood, or other details about the physical world, and they can be used with or without dialogue tags. Think about your mannerisms when you have conversations with people. Chances are you don't stand perfectly still while you talk. Adding in action beats can help make your dialogue more believable and remind readers of the setting.

Here are a few more examples of how action beats can be used:

Tom looked across the table, pausing until the waiter refilled his water. "Dina, I don't think that is necessary," he said under his breath.

"Let me see that again," Sarah said, reaching for the map. She spread it across the table. "The way I see it, we have one chance to get this right."

Evan barged into the room. "This meeting is a farce!" He marched to the podium. "Everything these men have told you so far is wrong."

Words and phrases to avoid

LET'S FACE IT, some words and phrases are just worn out! Scour your novel for any of these common offenders and see if you can replace them with a stronger choice instead. **Tip:** You can search most word processor documents by typing CTRL+F and a "Find" box will pop up. Just type in the word you want to find, and you will get a list of everywhere that word appears in your document. It's pretty cool, especially when searching through a whole novel.

Don't use this...	Write this instead...
seemed	
Jamal seemed sad.	Jamal hung his head and inched his way through the busy hallway. His bag weighed him down, full of books and burdens.
Kai seemed confused.	Randy shook his head. Why would Sheila act like that?
decided	
Wanda decided she liked Harry after all.	Wanda grabbed Harry and gave him a big kiss.
felt	
The dog felt scared.	The dog backed into the corner, its head bent low, his tail tucked between his legs.
thing	
The dishwasher's thing broke again.	The dishwasher rack broke again. (Always choose a specific word over a vague one.)

Don't use this...	Write this instead...

heard

Manny heard the birds outside his window before the sun even came up.	In the dark, Manny pulled the pillow over his ears. Why did those birds have to be so loud so early?

some (this includes all its relatives such as something, somewhere, etc.)

Some people would be at the party and bring something to share.	Jake, Susan, and Rob would be at the party and bring appetizers to share. (Whenever possible, choose specific words over vague words like some.)

was (to be verbs –is, was, etc.– especially paired with –ing words)

Leon was dancing all alone.	Leon danced all alone. ("To be" verbs are guilty of weakening many a sentence that could be stronger.)

adverbs (words ending in ly that usually describe the way an action is performed)

Tim ran quickly across the lawn.	Tim bolted across the lawn. (Limit your adverbs and find a stronger, more specific verb instead.)

very + most any word There is always a better word

very big	Huge, immense, giant
very sad	Depressed, grief-stricken (or even better, show the character being sad)
very cold	Freezing
very tired	Exhausted
very angry	Livid, enraged
very hungry	Ravenous

RABBIT HOLE IDEAS

SOMETIMES, LIKE ALICE following the white rabbit in *Alice in Wonderland*, you have ideas that leap across your mind that you are excited to follow. This is great! Don't run too far after them and abandon your book, but jot them down here for safe-keeping. It's always tempting to follow a new idea when the going gets tough (and trust me, when you write a novel, the going *will* get tough). Stay committed to your book, and it will give you the satisfaction of completing something!

That said, there is nothing wrong with writing a few of your other ideas and tucking them safely away for another day. When you are done with your book or need a short story idea for school, you can dive into those rabbit holes and see where they take you.

If you found this book helpful,
I would be incredibly grateful if you took a few
moments to leave a review on Amazon.

Thank you!

Sources

From Introduction

Korman, Gordan. (n.d.). About Gordan Korman. Retrieved from https://gordonkorman.com/more-resources/about-gordon-korman-2

Paolini, Christopher. (n.d.). Retrieved from https://www.paolini.net/biographies/christopher-paolini-full/

From Step 1 "Coming up with a Story Idea"

50 Awesome Quotes on the Power of Ideas. (2010, November 9). The Heart of Innovation. Retrieved October 14, 2021, from http://www.ideachampions.com/weblogs/archives/2010/11/50_very_awesome.shtml

Collins, B. (n.d.). *68 Inspiring Creativity Quotes To Spark Fresh Thinking*. Become a Writer Today. Retrieved October 14, 2021, from https://becomeawritertoday.com/creativity-quotes/

From Step 7 "Break up the Chapters into Scenes"

55 Motivational Writing Quotes from Famous Authors. (2019, January 30). Freewrite. Retrieved October 15, 2021, from https://getfreewrite.com/blogs/writing-success/55-motivational-writing-quotes

From Step 9 "Write good dialogue"

Carroll, L. (1991). *Alice in Wonderland*. Project Gutenberg. https://www.gutenberg.org/cache/epub/11/pg11-images.html#chap05

Craiker, K. N. (2020, May 19). *Action Beats: The Author's Multi-Tool*.

https://Prowritingaid.Com/Art/1139/Action-Beats-for-Authors.Aspx. Retrieved October 20, 2021, from https://prowritingaid.com/art/1139/action-beats-for-authors.aspx

Grahame, K. (1995). *The Wind in the Willows*. Project Gutenberg. https://www.gutenberg.org/files/289/289-h/289-h.htm#chap02

McKittrick Ros, A. (2010). *Irene Iddesleigh*. Project Gutenberg. https://www.gutenberg.org/cache/epub/34181/pg34181-images.html#chapIII

Using Beats to Bring Your Dialogue to Life: Turn the Beat Around. (2013, April 22). BookBaby. Retrieved October 20, 2021, from https://blog.bookbaby.com/2013/04/using-beats-to-bring-your-dialogue-to-life-turn-the-beat-around/

Van Dyne, E. (2016). *The Flying Girl*. Project Gutenberg. https://www.gutenberg.org/cache/epub/53386/pg53386-images.html#ch18

From Step 13 "Publish your book"

Book Cover Design Software: The Best Paid and Free DIY Apps. (2019, September 6). Reedsy Blog. Retrieved October 25, 2021, from https://blog.reedsy.com/book-cover-design-software/

Friedman, J. (2020, January 17). *The Complete Guide to Query Letters*. Jane Friedman. Retrieved October 29, 2021, from https://www.janefriedman.com/query-letters/

From References

Patterson, A. (2012, June 14). *Avoid These 10 Verbs That Make You Tell*. Writers Write. Retrieved October 16, 2021, from https://www.writers-write.co.za/avoid-these-10-verbs-that-make-you-tell/

Patterson, A. (2013, October 11). *209 Words To Describe Touch – A Resource For Writers*. Writers Write. Retrieved October 18, 2021, from https://www.writerswrite.co.za/209-words-to-describe-touch/

Patterson, A. (2014, January 6). *45 Ways To Avoid Using The Word 'Very.'* Writers Write. Retrieved October 16, 2021, from http://www.writerswrite.co.za/45-ways-to-avoid-using-the-word-very/

Patterson, A. (2014, April 5). *Cheat Sheets For Writing Body Language*. Writers Write. Retrieved October 18, 2021, from https://www.writers-write.co.za/cheat-sheets-for-writing-body-language/

Patterson, A. (2019, May 23). *106 Ways To Describe Sounds – A Resource For Writers*. Writers Write. Retrieved October 18, 2021, from https://www.writerswrite.co.za/106-ways-to-describe-sounds/

Patterson, A. (2019, June 10). *75 Words That Describe Smells – A Resource For Writers*. Writers Write. Retrieved October 18, 2021, from https://www.writerswrite.co.za/75-words-that-describe-smells/

Bunting, J. (2021, April 30). *7 Words to Avoid in Writing to Be a Better Writer*. The Write Practice. Retrieved October 16, 2021, from https://thewritepractice.com/better-writer-now/

IMPORTANT WORKSHEETS

(you'll refer back to these pages as you write your novel)

Index

A

Act 1 63-64, 66, 76, 89-90, 92-93, 168
  beginning 66, 76, 90, 93
  call to action 64, 66, 76, 90, 93
  inciting incident 64, 66, 76, 90, 93
  opening 64, 66, 76, 90, 92
  setup 64, 66, 76, 90, 92
Act 2 63, 65, 68, 70, 78, 80, 89, 90-91, 94-97, 96
  attack and bad guys regroup 65, 70, 80, 91, 96
  dark moment 65, 70, 80, 91, 96
  middle 68, 78, 90
  midpoint 65, 68, 78, 90, 95
  right after the middle 70, 80
  the choice 65, 68, 78, 90, 94
  try/fail 65, 68, 78, 90, 94
  turning point 65, 70, 80, 91, 97, 98
Act 3 63, 65, 72, 82, 91, 98-99, 168
  new plan 65, 72, 82, 91, 98
  climax 65, 72, 82, 91, 98-99
  end 63, 72, 82, 91, 98-99, 155
  resolution 65, 72, 82, 91, 99
Action 107
Action beats 122-123, 201-202
Alice in Wonderland 129, 207
Antagonist 64, 72, 82, 118
  see also villain

C

Chapter outline 89-99
  worksheets 102-103
Chapters 85, 90-91
  chapter beginnings 88
  scenes 100, 102, 104-105
  transitions 88, 101, 108
Character profiles 30-45
  2nd character profile 34-37
  3rd character profile 38-41
  4th character profile 42-45
  main character profile 30-33

Exercises and Prompts

Made in the USA
Las Vegas, NV
06 August 2024